Company's Coming®

KIDS COOKING

by
Jean Paré

D1041803

Dedication

Fun never tasted so good.

Back Cover Photo

1. Laryn Lovig
2. Lance Paré
3. Christy Lovig
4. Carla Lovig
5. Quentin Paré
6. Jennifer MacPherson
7. Shawna Luco
8. Gramma (Jean Paré)
9. Raylene Sweeney *
10. Shalene Sweeney
11. Kalyca Luco *
12. Lane Lovig
13. Michelle Paré
14. Landon Lovig
15. Keltie Hruba
16. Keagan Lovig *
17. Amanda Lovig
18. Michael MacPherson
19. Tina Lovig
20. Jordon Lovig
21. James MacPherson
22. Kerri Ann Lovig
23. Reagan Lovig

* Great Grandchild

Front Cover Photo

1. Sugar Cookies page 38
2. Ginger Crinkles page 37
3. Peanut Butter Gems page 40
4. Crispy Roll page 102
5. Macaroni Magic page 66
6. Jiffy Pizza page 98

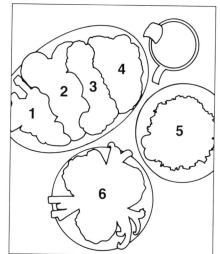

China Courtesy Of:
Chintz & Company

KIDS COOKING

Second Printing August 1995

ISBN 1-895455-44-8

Published and Distributed by
Company's Coming Publishing Limited
Box 8037, Station "F"
Edmonton, Alberta, Canada
T6H 4N9

**Published Simultaneously in
Canada and the United States of America**

Printed In Canada

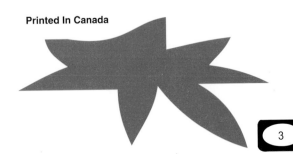

Welcome to the family

Company's Coming
Cookbooks

Table Of Contents

The Jean Paré Story

Jean Paré grew up understanding that the combination of family, friends and home cooking is the essence of a good life. Her years of experience as a professional caterer and mother of four led to an appreciation of quick and easy recipes using everyday ingredients.

In response to requests for her recipes, Jean published the first Company's Coming cookbook in 1981. It was an immediate best-seller. Now, with more than two dozen titles in print, sales of Company's Coming cookbooks have surpassed 10 million copies!

Company's Coming cookbooks are distributed throughout Canada, the United States and overseas. The series is pub-lished in English, French and Spanish. A recent addition to the family is the smaller, more specialized series called Pint Size Books. Recipes found in these books continue in the familiar and trusted Company's Coming style.

All recipes are proven in our own test kitchen before appearing in a Company's Coming cookbook. A team of more than fifty dedicated people then ensure those recipes find their way into kitchens around the world.

Jean Paré continues to gain new supporters by adhering to what she calls: "the golden rule of cooking — never share a recipe you wouldn't use yourself". It's an approach that works 10 million times over!

Foreword

Kids Cooking will help you learn the basics of cooking and about the terms and equipment used in the kitchen.

Getting Started: To begin, wash your hands and put on an apron. Choose a recipe and read through it, then make sure the ingredients are on hand. If you are not familiar with a cooking term, look it up in the "Glossary" on pages 8 and 9. Next, gather the equipment you will need. Check the diagrams in the "Equipment And Utensils" section on pages 10 and 11. Spoon measurements are level. Dry ingredients such as flour or sugar are leveled off with the dull side of a knife or the handle of a spatula. Milk and other liquids are measured at eye level with the cup on a flat surface.

Safety: Kitchen safety is very important. Even if your hands are dry, never use an electric beater in a bowl that is in the kitchen sink. It is not safe. Never touch anything electrical with wet hands. Keep electric cords away from the sink as well as water or anything wet. Always pull out a plug by holding and pulling on the plug itself, not the cord. Sharp knives should be held by the handle with the cutting edge away from you. Keep the handles of saucepans turned inward on the stove to prevent bumping and spilling. Use oven mitts (or pot holders) when handling hot dishes. Turn off burners and oven and unplug small appliances when not in use. Clean up as you go and be sure to ask for help from an adult if you need it!

What To Cook: Why not start by making your school lunch? Check the section called "Bag Lunches" on page 116 for ideas. For an easy supper try Spaghetti Dish or Macaroni Magic. Fruit Pizza makes a great dessert or a special get-together treat. Make Nachos for those sudden hunger attacks. Whether you have cooked many times or this is your first cooking experience you will feel proud and thrilled when you serve and eat the recipes you've made!

Jean Paré

A Note To Parents

This book is intended for your children to use. Please supervise them when necessary. The handling of sharp knives, boiling liquids and hot pans needs to be considered carefully with younger children. Encourage them to begin by making a snack they love to eat. Then they can pick recipes to prepare a breakfast, lunch or evening meal.

Letting beginners explore and experience adventure in the kitchen will lead to a lifetime of cooking enjoyment!

Glossary

Bake - to cook in an oven preheated to the temperature it says in the recipe. Use either the bottom rack or center rack (see picture page 11).

Batter - a mixture of flour, liquid and other ingredients that can be thin (such as pancake batter) or thick (such as muffin batter).

Beat - to mix 2 or more ingredients with a spoon, fork or electric mixer, using a circular motion, until they are smooth.

Boil - to cook a liquid in a saucepan until bubbles rise in a steady pattern and break on the surface. Steam also starts to rise from the surface.

Broil - to cook under the top heating element in the oven. Use either the top rack or the upper rack (see picture page 11).

Break An Egg - Tap the side of the egg on the edge of a bowl or cup to crack the shell. Place the tips of both thumbs in the crack and open the shell.

Brown - to fry, broil or bake food in order to deepen the surface color, being careful not to burn the food.

Chill - to refrigerate until cold.

Chop - to cut food carefully into small pieces with a sharp knife on a cutting board; to chop finely is to cut foods as small as you can.

Combine - to put 2 or more ingredients together.

Cut In - to combine solid fat (such as butter or margarine) with dry ingredients (such as flour) using a fork or pastry blender until the mixture looks like big crumbs the size of green peas.

Dice - to cut food into small ¼ inch (0.5 cm) cube-shaped pieces.

Dip (into) - to lower into a liquid either part way or all the way.

Drain - to strain away an unwanted liquid (such as water or grease) using a colander or strainer. Do this over the kitchen sink. Ask an adult for help, as a large saucepan of water can be very heavy. Drain grease into a metal can and throw away in the garbage after it hardens.

Drizzle - to dribble drops of glaze or icing over food in a random manner from tines of a fork or the end of a spoon.

Fold - to mix gently using a rubber spatula by cutting down in the center and lifting towards the edge of the bowl. Use a down, up, over movement, turning the bowl as you repeat.

Garnish - to decorate food with edible condiments such as parsley sprigs, fruit slices or vegetable cut-outs.

Grease - to rub the inside bottom and sides of a baking pan with butter, margarine or cooking oil, or spray with no-stick cooking spray, to keep foods from sticking to the pan.

Grease And Flour - (see Grease). Cover the grease with a light coating of flour.

Heat - to make something warm or hot by placing the pan on the stove burner that is turned on to the level it says in the recipe.

Knead - to work dough into a smooth putty-like mass by pressing and folding using the heels of your hands.

Let Stand - to let a baked product cool down slightly on a wire rack or hot pad, while still in its baking pan.

Mash - to squash cooked or very ripe foods with a fork or potato masher.

Melt - to heat a solid food such as butter, margarine, cheese or chocolate, until it turns into a liquid. Be careful not to burn it.

Mix - (see Combine)

Mixing Just Until Moistened - to put dry ingredients with liquid ingredients until dry ingredients are just wet. Mixture will still be lumpy.

Process - to mix up or cut up in a blender (or food processor) until it is the way it says in the recipe.

Rounded Teaspoonful/Tablespoonful - to mound ingredient or dough slightly in the measuring spoon asked for in the recipe.

Scramble-Fry - to brown ground meat in hot oil or other fat using a spoon, fork or pancake lifter to break up the meat into small crumb-like pieces as it cooks.

Scrape - to use a rubber spatula to remove as much of a mixture as possible from inside a bowl or saucepan.

Simmer - to cook liquids in a saucepan over a very low heat on the stove burner so that slow bubbles appear on the surface around the sides of the liquid.

Slice - to cut foods such as apples, carrots, tomatoes, meat or bread into thin sections or pieces, using a sharp knife.

Spoon (into) - to move ingredients from one container to another, using a spoon to scoop from one and drop into the other.

Spread - to cover the surface of one product (generally a more solid food) with another product (generally a softer food such as icing or butter).

Stir - to mix 2 or more ingredients with a spoon, using a circular motion.

Toast - to brown lightly in a toaster or frying pan or under the broiler in the oven.

Toss - to mix salad ingredients lightly with a lifting motion, using two forks, two spoons or salad tongs.

Turn (onto) - to remove a baked product from its pan by loosening the edges and turning the pan upside down, carefully letting the product fall out onto a wire rack, cutting board or serving plate.

Equipment And Utensils

 Blender

 Broiler Pan

 Bundt Pan

 Biscuit Cutter

 Casserole Dish

 Colander

 Cookie Cutters

 Cookie Sheet

 Cutting Board

 Table Fork   Table Knife

 Double Boiler

 Dutch Oven

 Electric Frying Pan

Electric Mixer

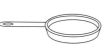 Frying Pan

Fudgesicle or Popsicle Molds

 Grater

 Hot Pad

 Ice Cream Scoop

 Jelly Roll Pan or Baking Sheet

 Loaf Pan

 Dry Measuring Cups

 Liquid Measuring Cups

 Measuring Spoons

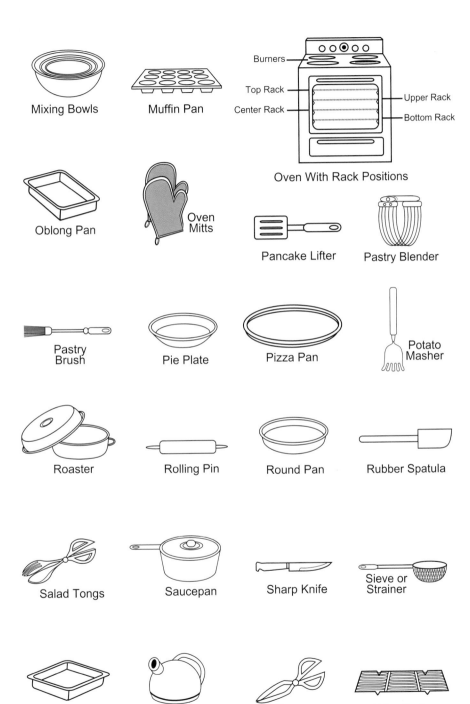

Mixing Bowls

Muffin Pan

Burners

Top Rack
Center Rack

Upper Rack
Bottom Rack

Oven With Rack Positions

Oblong Pan

Oven Mitts

Pancake Lifter

Pastry Blender

Pastry Brush

Pie Plate

Pizza Pan

Potato Masher

Roaster

Rolling Pin

Round Pan

Rubber Spatula

Salad Tongs

Saucepan

Sharp Knife

Sieve or Strainer

Square Pan

Tea Kettle

Tongs

Wire Rack

Vanilla Milk Shake

An all-time favorite. Start with this basic shake, then pick a favorite from the others. Do not freeze.

1.

Rounded scoops of vanilla ice cream	**2**	**2**
Cold milk	**¾ cup**	**175 mL**
Instant vanilla pudding powder (optional) (see Note)	**1 tbsp.**	**15 mL**
Vanilla flavoring	**½ tsp.**	**2 mL**

You will need: a blender, an ice cream scoop, measuring spoons, measuring cups, a tall glass and a drinking straw.

1. Place all of the ingredients in the blender. Hold the lid on the blender. Process for about 20 seconds or until smooth and frothy. Serve in the glass with the straw. Makes about 2 cups (500 mL).

CHOCOLATE MILK SHAKE: Leave out the vanilla flavoring. Add 2 tbsp. (30 mL) chocolate syrup.

STRAWBERRY MILK SHAKE: Leave out the vanilla flavoring. Increase the milk to 1 cup (250 mL) and add ½ cup (125 mL) of sliced strawberries. Strawberry ice cream can also be used instead of the vanilla ice cream.

ORANGE MILK SHAKE: Leave out the vanilla flavoring and the milk. Add 1 cup (250 mL) of orange soft drink.

CHOCO BANANA MILK SHAKE: Leave out the vanilla flavoring. Add 2 tbsp. (30 mL) chocolate syrup and 1 ripe banana, peeled and sliced.

PURPLE COW: Leave out the vanilla flavoring. Add ½ cup (125 mL) grape soft drink.

Note: The pudding powder helps to keep the shake thick.

All pictured on page 13.

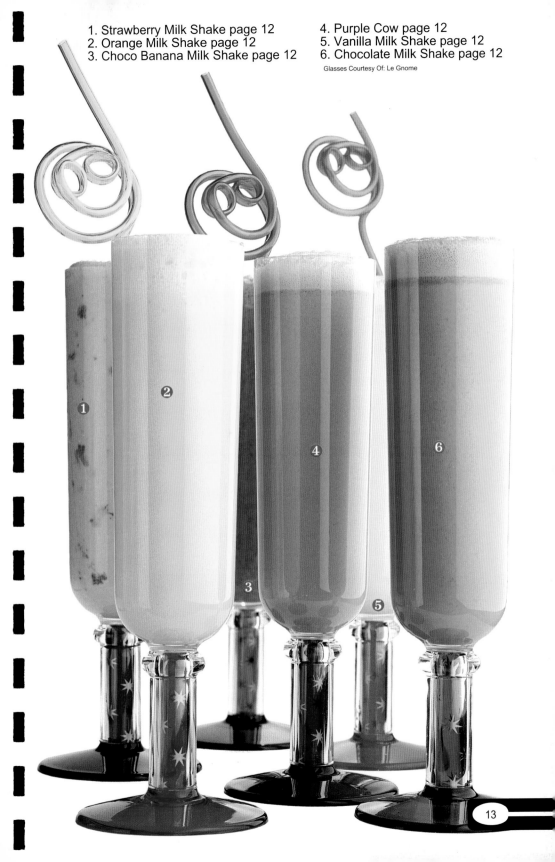

1. Strawberry Milk Shake page 12
2. Orange Milk Shake page 12
3. Choco Banana Milk Shake page 12
4. Purple Cow page 12
5. Vanilla Milk Shake page 12
6. Chocolate Milk Shake page 12

Root Beer Float/Soda

Whether you call this a float or a soda, it is a cinch to make any flavor you want. Do not freeze.

1. Rounded scoops vanilla ice cream	**2**	**2**
Cold root beer, to fill glass		

You will need: an ice cream scoop, a tall soda glass, a long-handled spoon and a drinking straw.

1. Put the ice cream into the tall glass. Pour the root beer over the ice cream to fill the glass. Add the spoon and/or the drinking straw to the glass. Makes 1 large drink.

Variation: Use any other flavors of your favorite soft drink.

1. Root Beer Float
2. Orange Float

Soda Glasses Courtesy Of:
Le Gnome

Punch Bowl Set Courtesy Of:
The Enchanted Kitchen

Party Punch

A smooth fruit punch. Do not freeze.

1. Concentrated frozen orange juice, thawed	**6 oz.**	**170 mL**
Concentrated frozen lemonade, thawed	**6 oz.**	**170 mL**
Pineapple juice	**2 cups**	**500 mL**
2. Ginger ale	**4 cups**	**1 L**
3. Ice cubes, per glass	**2-3**	**2-3**

You will need: a large 2 quart (2 L) pitcher or small punch bowl, measuring cups, a long-handled mixing spoon and regular glasses or punch cups.

1. Empty the concentrated orange juice and the concentrated lemonade into the pitcher. Pour in the pineapple juice. Stir until mixed well. Place the punch in the refrigerator to keep cold until you are ready to use it.

2. Add the ginger ale to the pitcher. Stir lightly. If using a punch bowl, empty the juices from the pitcher into the bowl. Add the ginger ale. Stir lightly just to mix.

3. Put 2 or 3 ice cubes in each glass or punch cup. Fill with punch. Garnish with maraschino cherries, a slice of orange, tiny umbrellas or plastic ice cubes. Makes 7½ cups (1.75 L), enough for ten 6 oz. (175 mL) drinks.

Pictured above.

Pink Punch

Pretty color with a zippy flavor. Do not freeze.

1.	**Bottled cranberry cocktail juice**	**2 cups**	**500 mL**
	Prepared orange juice	**2 cups**	**500 mL**
2.	**Ginger ale**	**2 cups**	**500 mL**
	Ice cubes, per glass	**2-3**	**2-3**

You will need: a 2 quart (2 L) pitcher, measuring cups, a long-handled mixing spoon and glasses.

1. Combine both juices in the pitcher. Stir. Chill in the refrigerator.

2. When you are ready to serve the punch, add the ginger ale and stir lightly. Place the ice cubes in each glass. Pour the punch over the ice cubes. Makes 6 cups (1.5 L), enough for 4 or 5 servings.

Mock Champagne

A fine-tasting bubbly drink, almost like the real thing! Do not freeze.

1. Bottled white grape juice, chilled	4 cups	1 L
Club soda, chilled	4 cups	1 L
2. Ice cubes, per glass	2-3	2-3
Lime or lemon slices, for garnish	10	10

You will need: a 2 quart (2 L) pitcher, measuring cups, a long-handled mixing spoon, tall glasses and a sharp knife.

1. Pour the grape juice into the pitcher and chill in the refrigerator for about 2 hours. Immediately before serving, pour the club soda into the grape juice. Stir lightly.

2. Place some ice cubes in each glass. Fill with the drink mixture. Use the knife to make a cut from the center of the lime or lemon slices through the outside of the rind. Fit over the edge of each glass. Makes about ten 6 oz. (175 mL) servings.

Pictured below.

Glasses Courtesy Of: Le Gnome

Hot Cocoa

Easy to make for yourself but you can also make it for your friends.

1. Cocoa	1½ tsp.	7 mL
Granulated sugar	1½ tsp.	7 mL
Water	1½ tsp.	7 mL
2. Milk	¾ cup	175 mL
3. Miniature marshmallows, or frozen whipped topping	3-4	3-4

You will need: measuring spoons, measuring cups, a small mixing spoon, a mug that holds 1 cup (250 mL) and a small saucepan.

1. Mix the cocoa, sugar and water in the mug until smooth.

2. Pour the milk into the saucepan. Heat on medium until hot. Stir slowly to make sure it does not burn, then carefully pour the milk into the mug. Stir.

3. Top with the marshmallows or some whipped topping, if you would like. Serves 1.

Pictured below.

Hot Chocolate Drink

With the Hot Chocolate Mix on hand, you can make a cup of hot chocolate in a hurry.

1. HOT CHOCOLATE MIX

Powdered milk	2 cups	500 mL
Granulated sugar	²/₃ cup	150 mL
Cocoa	½ cup	125 mL
Salt	¼ tsp.	1 mL

2. FOR ONE MUG

Prepared Hot Chocolate Mix	3 tbsp.	45 mL
Boiling water	¾ cup	175 mL

3. Miniature marshmallows, or frozen whipped topping — 3-4   3-4

You will need: a medium bowl, a mixing spoon, measuring cups, measuring spoons, a container with a lid, a 1 cup (250 mL) mug, a tea kettle and a small spoon.

1. Hot Chocolate Mix: Combine the powdered milk, sugar, cocoa and salt in the bowl. Stir until mixed well and no lumps remain. Spoon into the container. Cover with the lid. Store in the kitchen cupboard. Makes 2½ cups (625 mL), enough for about 12 hot drinks.

2. For One Mug: Put the Hot Chocolate Mix into the mug. Add the boiling water. Stir well until all the mix dissolves into the boiling water.

3. Top with the marshmallows or some whipped topping, if you would like. Serves 1.

Choco Banana Loaf

A tasty combination of favorite flavors.

1. Butter or hard margarine,   ½ cup   125 mL
   softened (at room temperature)
   Granulated sugar   1 cup   250 mL
   Large eggs   2   2
   Vanilla flavoring   1 tsp.   5 mL

2. Ripe medium bananas   3   3
   Milk   ¼ cup   50 mL

3. All-purpose flour   1½ cups   375mL
   Cocoa   ¼ cup   50 mL
   Baking powder   1½ tsp.   7 mL
   Baking soda   ½ tsp.   2 mL
   Salt   ¼ tsp.   1 mL

4. Chopped walnuts   ½ cup   125 mL

(continued on next page)

You will need: a 9 x 5 x 3 inch (22 x 12 x 7 cm) loaf pan, a medium bowl, a mixing spoon, an electric mixer, measuring spoons, measuring cups, a table fork, a table knife, oven mitts and a wire rack.

1. Turn the oven on to 350°F (175°C). Grease the loaf pan. Combine the butter or margarine, sugar, eggs and vanilla flavoring in the bowl. Beat on medium speed, just until moistened.

2. Mash enough of the the bananas with the fork to make 1 cup (250 mL). Add to the batter in the bowl along with the milk. Beat on low speed to blend in. (Eat any leftover banana.)

3. Add the next 5 ingredients. Beat on low speed until the flour mixture is moistened.

4. Use the spoon to stir in the walnuts. Turn the batter into the loaf pan. Bake on the center rack in the oven for 50 to 60 minutes. A wooden toothpick inserted in the center of the loaf should come out clean and dry. Use the oven mitts to remove the pan to the wire rack. Let stand for 15 minutes. Cut around the sides with the knife to loosen. Turn the pan upside down onto the wire rack to remove the loaf. Turn the loaf right side up. Cool completely. Store the loaf in a plastic bag. This slices more easily when it is 1 day old. Makes 1 loaf.

Fun Buns

A bit fussy but not difficult to make. They disappear fast.

1.	**All-purpose flour**	**2 cups**	**450 mL**
	Granulated sugar	**3 tbsp.**	**45 mL**
	Baking powder	**4 tsp.**	**20 mL**
	Cream of tartar	**½ tsp.**	**2 mL**
	Salt	**½ tsp.**	**2 mL**
2.	**Cold butter or hard margarine**	**¼ cup**	**60 mL**
3.	**Cold milk**	**¾ cup**	**175 mL**
4.	**COATING**		
	Brown sugar, packed	**6 tbsp.**	**90 mL**
	Ground cinnamon	**2 tsp.**	**10 mL**
5.	**Butter or hard margarine**	**1 tbsp.**	**15 mL**

You will need: a medium bowl, 2 mixing spoons, measuring spoons, measuring cups, a pastry blender, a sharp knife, a small bowl, a small saucepan, a hot pad, a pastry brush, a cookie sheet, oven mitts and a wire rack.

1. Turn the oven on to 400°F (205°C). Measure the first 5 ingredients in the medium bowl. Stir well.

2. Add the butter or hard margarine and cut it in with the pastry blender until it is in tiny pieces and the whole mixture is crumbly.

3. Add the milk. Stir until it pulls away from the side of the bowl and forms a soft ball. Turn out onto a lightly floured surface. Knead 8 times or until dough is smooth. Cut the dough into 2 equal portions. Cut each portion in half making 4 pieces of dough. Now divide each piece into 3, making a total of 12 pieces. Using the palms of your hands, roll each piece into a long rope at least 12 inches (30 cm) long.

(continued on next page)

Bowl and Spreader Courtesy Of:
Le Gnome

4. Coating: Measure the brown sugar and cinnamon into the small bowl. Stir well until evenly mixed. Pour onto working surface. Spread into a rectangle about 4 x 14 inches (10 x 40 cm).

5. Put the second amount of butter or margarine into the small saucepan over medium heat until it melts. Remove the saucepan to the hot pad. Use the pastry brush to brush another rectangle on the working surface, the same size as the sugar-cinnamon. Roll 1 rope at a time in the butter or margarine, then roll it in the sugar-cinnamon to coat. Roll up like a spiral or pin-wheel, like a snake might curl up. Pinch the last ½ inch (12 mm) of the end flat and tuck it underneath the bun. Arrange the buns on the greased cookie sheet. Bake on the center rack in the oven for 12 to 15 minutes. A wooden toothpick inserted in the center should come out clean. Use the oven mitts to remove the baking sheet to the wire rack. Cool. Makes 12 buns.

Pictured below.

Platter Courtesy Of:
The Bay Housewares Dept.

Germ Muffins

The germ that makes it so good and so healthy is wheat germ.

1.
Large egg	1	1
Granulated sugar	1/3 cup	75 mL
Brown sugar, packed	1/3 cup	75 mL
Cooking oil	1/3 cup	75 mL
Buttermilk (see Note)	1 cup	250 mL
Vanilla flavoring	1 tsp.	5 mL

2.
All-purpose flour	1¼ cups	300 mL
Wheat germ	1 cup	250 mL
Baking powder	1 tsp.	5 mL
Baking soda	1 tsp.	5 mL
Salt	¼ tsp.	1 mL

You will need: a muffin pan, a large bowl, 2 mixing spoons, measuring spoons, measuring cups, a medium bowl, oven mitts and a wire rack.

1. Turn the oven on to 400°F (205°C). Grease the muffin pan. Break the egg into the large bowl. Add both of the sugars, the cooking oil, buttermilk and vanilla flavoring. Mix well.

2. In the medium bowl place the next 5 ingredients. Stir to mix. Pour the wet mixture over the dry mixture. Stir just until moistened. Do not stir too much. Spoon the batter into the muffin pan filling each cup ¾ full. Bake on the center rack in the oven for about 12 minutes. A wooden toothpick inserted in the center of 2 or 3 muffins should come out clean. Use the oven mitts to remove the muffin pan to the wire rack. Let stand for 10 minutes then remove the muffins to the rack to cool. Makes 12 muffins.

Variation: Add ½ cup (125 mL) raisins or chopped dates or blueberries.

Note: Instead of Buttermilk, add 1 tbsp. (15 mL) white vinegar plus milk to make 1 cup (250 mL).

Bran Biscuits

A delicious warm biscuit like this goes with any meal of the day. Also makes a great snack.

1. **All bran cereal, 100% (not bran flakes)**	**1 cup**	**250 mL**
Milk	**1 cup**	**250 mL**
2. **Biscuit mix**	**2¼ cups**	**550 mL**

You will need: a medium bowl, measuring cups, a mixing spoon, a rolling pin, a biscuit cutter, a cookie sheet, oven mitts and a wire rack.

1. Turn the oven on to 425°F (220°C). Put the cereal and the milk into the bowl. Stir. Let the mixture stand for 10 minutes to soften the cereal.

2. Add the biscuit mix. Stir until it forms a ball of dough. Put the dough on a lightly floured surface. Knead gently 8 times or until dough is smooth. Pat or roll the dough about ¾ inch (2 cm) thick. Cut into 2 inch (5 cm) rounds. If you don't have a biscuit cutter, use a water glass turned upside down. Arrange on the ungreased cookie sheet. Bake on the center rack in the oven for 12 to 15 minutes until they are risen and browned. Use the oven mitts to remove the cookie sheet to the wire rack. Serve warm. Makes 16 biscuits.

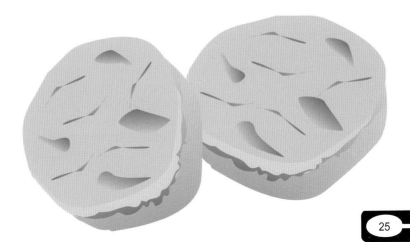

Pancakes

Start the day right or even enjoy these for lunch or supper. Try a creative design, as above.

1.	**Large eggs**	**2**	**2**
2.	**Milk**	**1 cup**	**250 mL**
	Cooking oil	**2 tbsp.**	**30 mL**
3.	**All-purpose flour**	**1¼ cups**	**300 mL**
	Granulated sugar	**1 tbsp.**	**15 mL**
	Baking powder	**1 tbsp.**	**15 mL**
	Salt	**¼ tsp.**	**1 mL**

You will need: a small bowl, measuring spoons, measuring cups, a mixing spoon, a frying pan, no-stick cooking spray, a pancake lifter and a serving spoon.

1. Break the eggs into the bowl and stir until the eggs are fairly smooth and a bit bubbly.

2. Add the milk and cooking oil to the eggs. Mix.

3. Add all the remaining ingredients. Stir just until moistened. Heat the frying pan until a few drops of water bounce all over. An electric frying pan would be 380°F (190°C). Spray the pan with no-stick cooking spray. Scoop spoonfuls of the batter onto the frying pan using the serving spoon. When tops are bubbly and the edges are a bit dry looking, turn them to brown the other sides. Spray should not be needed for the rest of the cooking. Remove with the lifter to a plate. Serve with butter or margarine and syrup. Makes 18 round pancakes.

French Toast

Serve with maple syrup. A scrumptious breakfast. Pictured below.

1. **Large egg**	1	1
Milk or water	3 tbsp.	45 mL
Salt	$\frac{1}{8}$ tsp.	0.5 mL
Vanilla flavoring	$\frac{1}{8}$ tsp.	0.5 mL
2. **Hard margarine (butter browns too fast)**	2 tsp.	10 mL
3. **French bread slices, 1 inch, (2.5 cm) thick**	2-3	2-3
4. **Icing (confectioner's) sugar, sprinkle**		

You will need: a pie plate, a fork, measuring spoons, measuring cups, a frying pan, a pancake lifter, a sieve and a large dinner plate.

1. Break the egg into the pie plate. Beat with the fork. Add the milk or water, salt and vanilla flavoring. Beat with the fork to mix.

2. Melt the margarine in the medium-hot frying pan.

3. Dip the bread slices, 1 at a time, into the egg mixture, turning to coat both sides. Brown both sides in the frying pan. Cut the slices in half. Transfer to the large plate.

4. Put a spoonful of icing sugar into the sieve. Shake it lightly over top of the slices to give a light sprinkle. Serves 1 or 2.

FRENCH TOAST TWIST: Make an ordinary peanut butter and jam or a peanut butter and honey sandwich. Continue from Step 3. above.

Plate Courtesy Of:
The Bay Housewares Dept.

Framed Eggs

A picturesque way to serve eggs. Do not freeze.

1. **Bread slice, 1 inch (2.5 cm)**   **1**   **1**
      thick, buttered on both sides
      (see Note)

2. **Butter or hard margarine**   **½ tsp.**   **2 mL**
      Large egg   **1**   **1**
      Salt, sprinkle
      Pepper, sprinkle

You will need: a frying pan with a lid, a water glass, measuring spoons and a pancake lifter.

1. Heat the frying pan to medium. Using the water glass turned upside down, press to cut a round piece out of the center of the bread. Place both the bread slice and the round piece of bread in the frying pan. Brown 1 side. Turn heat to medium-low. Turn the bread slice and the round piece of bread over.

2. Melt the butter or margarine in the hole in the bread slice. Break the egg into the hole. Sprinkle with salt and pepper. Put the lid on. Cook slowly until the white of the egg is set. Remove the egg and toast with the lifter to the plate. Garnish with the toasted round piece and fresh fruit and cheese. Makes 1 serving.

Pictured above.

Note: If you want to use an ordinary bread slice, brown one side of the bread slice and the round piece of bread, then remove both from the pan. Break the egg into the pan. Put the unbrowned side of the bread slice over the egg, centering the hole over the yolk. At the same time place the round piece of bread, untoasted side down, in the frying pan and brown the other side. Cover with the lid and cook slowly until the white of the egg is set.

Sour Cream Pound Cake

This a solid heavier cake. Add a scoop of ice cream and Butterscotch Sauce, page 47, over each slice for a delicious dessert.

1.			
	Butter or hard margarine, softened (at room temperature)	²/₃ cup	150 mL
	Granulated sugar	2 cups	450 mL
	Large eggs	4	4
	Vanilla flavoring	1 tsp.	5 mL
2.	All-purpose flour	2 cups	450 mL
	Salt	¹/₄ tsp.	1 mL
	Baking soda	¹/₄ tsp.	1 mL
3.	Sour cream	²/₃ cup	150 mL

You will need: a 12 cup (2.7 L) bundt pan, a large bowl, measuring spoons, measuring cups, an electric mixer, a mixing spoon, a rubber spatula, oven mitts and a wire rack.

1. Turn the oven on to 325°F (160°C). Grease and flour the bundt pan. Combine the butter or margarine and sugar in the bowl. Beat on low speed to break up. Beat in the eggs 1 at a time on medium speed. Add the vanilla flavoring. Stir.

2. Stir in the flour, salt and baking soda.

3. Add the sour cream. Stir until it is mixed in. Scrape the batter into the prepared pan. Bake on the center rack in the oven for about 55 minutes. A wooden toothpick inserted in the center of the cake should come out clean. Use the oven mitts to remove the pan to the wire rack. Let stand for 15 minutes. Turn the cake out onto the rack to finish cooling. Makes 1 cake.

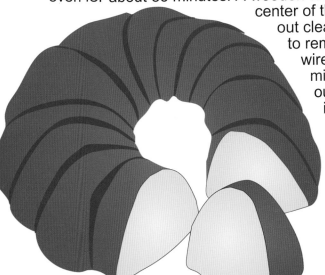

Tomato Soup Cake

An old fashioned cake that is prepared in one bowl all at one time.

1. Butter or hard margarine,

Butter or hard margarine, softened (at room temperature)	**6 tbsp.**	**90 mL**
Condensed tomato soup	**10 oz.**	**284 mL**
All-purpose flour	**1½ cups**	**375 mL**
Granulated sugar	**1 cup**	**250 mL**
Large egg	**1**	**1**
Baking soda	**1 tsp.**	**5 mL**
Cinnamon	**1 tsp.**	**5 mL**
Ground allspice	**¼ tsp.**	**1 mL**
Salt	**¼ tsp.**	**1 mL**
2. Raisins (optional)	**¾ cup**	**175 mL**

You will need: a large bowl, an electric mixer, measuring spoons, measuring cups, a rubber spatula, a 9 x 9 inch (22 x 22 cm) pan, oven mitts and a wire rack.

1. Turn the oven on to 350°F (175°C). Measure the first 9 ingredients into the bowl. Beat on low speed until the flour is moistened, then beat on medium speed until the batter is smooth. Scrape the sides of the bowl 2 or 3 times with the rubber spatula while beating. After the batter is smooth, scrape the batter off the beaters into the bowl.

2. Add the raisins. Stir to distribute them. Grease the inside of the pan. Turn the batter into the pan. Bake on the center rack in the oven for about 35 minutes. A wooden toothpick inserted in the center of the cake should come out clean. Use the oven mitts to remove the cake pan to the wire rack. Cool. Ice with Cream Cheese Icing, page 31. Makes 1 cake.

Pictured on page 31.

1. Tomato Soup Cake page 30
2. Cream Cheese Icing

Plate Courtesy Of:
The Bay China Dept.

Cream Cheese Icing

Creamy and yummy, as pictured above.

1.			
Cream cheese, softened (at room temperature)		4 oz.	125 g
Butter or hard margarine, softened (at room temperature)		2 tbsp.	30 mL
Icing (confectioner's) sugar		1½ cups	375 mL
Vanilla flavoring		½ tsp.	2 mL

You will need: a small bowl, measuring spoons, measuring cups and an electric mixer.

1. Combine the cream cheese, butter or margarine, icing sugar and vanilla flavoring in the bowl. Beat on low speed until moistened then beat on medium speed until smooth and fluffy. Spread over Tomato Soup Cake, page 30, or your favorite cake. Makes 1¼ cups (300 mL), enough to ice a 9 x 9 inch (22 x 22 cm) cake.

31

 # Turtle Chocolates

Nutty and chewy. Invite your friends over to help you make these.

1.	**Caramels, light brown**	**48**	**48**
	Milk	**3 tbsp.**	**45 mL**
2.	**Chopped pecans**	**2 cups**	**500 mL**
3.	**COATING**		
	Semisweet chocolate chips	**2 cups**	**500 mL**
	Grated paraffin wax, lightly packed	**6 tbsp.**	**100 mL**

You will need: 2 heavy medium saucepans, measuring spoons, measuring cups, 2 mixing spoons, a cookie sheet, waxed paper, a hot pad and a table fork.

1. Unwrap the caramels and put them into one of the saucepans. Add the milk. Place over low heat. Stir often until the caramels are melted.

2. Cover the cookie sheet with the waxed paper. Grease the paper well. Add the pecans to the melted caramels. Stir. Leave on very low heat to keep from getting hard. Drop by rounded teaspoonfuls onto the waxed paper. Place in the refrigerator for 1 hour until firm.

3. Coating: Place the chocolate chips and paraffin wax in the second saucepan. Heat on low, stirring often, until melted and smooth. Remove the saucepan to the hot pad. Drop 1 clump of caramel mixture at a time into the chocolate. Slide the fork under the piece and lift up to let the excess chocolate drip back into the saucepan. Repeat with the remaining pieces. Place back on the waxed paper. Chill. Makes 3 to 3½ dozen chocolates.

Pictured below.

1. Turtle Chocolates
2. Marshmallow Delights
   page 33

Placemat And Plate Courtesy Of:
The Bay Housewares Dept.

Marshmallow Delights

These take extra time but are fun to make. If you want to keep any, freeze them in a container with a lid.

1.	**McIntosh toffee bars**	**3 × 2 oz.**	**3 × 56 g**
	Butter or hard margarine	**¼ cup**	**50 mL**
	Canned sweetened condensed milk	**⅔ cup**	**150 mL**
2.	**Special K cereal**	**4 cups**	**1 L**
	Marshmallows, large	**30-35**	**30-35**

You will need: a table knife, a double boiler, measuring cups, a medium bowl, a mixing spoon, a hot pad, a table fork, waxed paper and a rubber spatula.

1. Break up the toffee bars by placing one bar in the palm of your hand. Use the handle of the knife to hit it, cracking it. Put the pieces into the top of the double boiler. Add the butter or margarine. Add the milk. Put some hot water in the bottom of the double boiler. Set the top part in and put the double boiler on a medium-hot burner. Stir the toffee mixture occasionally until it is melted and smooth. Remove the double boiler to the hot pad. Keep the toffee mixture over the hot water.

2. Pour the Special K cereal into the bowl. Stick the fork into the end of one of the marshmallows. Roll it in the toffee mixture to coat the bottom end and sides. (The top end will be the end it rests on, the end you push off the fork with your fingers.) Hold the marshmallow over the toffee mixture to drain for a moment or two, then roll in the cereal. Use your other hand to help to cover it with the cereal. Push the coated marshmallow off the fork onto the waxed paper on the counter and turn it to stand on the uncoated end. Repeat with the rest of the marshmallows. If the toffee mixture gets stiff, heat the water underneath until it begins to boil again. Makes 30 to 35 marshmallow treats.

Pictured on page 32.

Peanut Chew

To make this last, you will have to put everyone on rations. It is so-o-o good. Just like my son's favorite candy bar.

1.	**Creamed honey**	**1 cup**	**250 mL**
	Semisweet chocolate chips	**2 cups**	**500 mL**
2.	**Smooth peanut butter**	**1 cup**	**250 mL**
3.	**Salted peanuts, chopped**	**2 cups**	**500 mL**

You will need: a 10 x 15 inch (25 x 38 cm) jelly roll pan, some aluminum foil, a large heavy saucepan, measuring cups, a mixing spoon, a hot pad, a rubber spatula, a cutting board and a sharp knife.

To get the jelly roll pan ready, tear off some foil longer than the pan. Run your hand under the tap to wet it, then rub over the inside of the bottom and sides of the pan to dampen. Center the foil over the pan. Press it in place, pressing into the corners as well. The damp pan makes the foil cling so it doesn't move around when you spread the candy bar mixture on it.

1. Combine the honey and chocolate chips in the saucepan. Place the pan on low heat until the chips start to melt. Stir often. Turn the heat to medium-high. Stir continually until the mixture starts to boil. Remove the saucepan to the hot pad.

2. Add the peanut butter. Stir until the mixture becomes smooth.

3. Add the peanuts. Stir until mixed well. Pour the mixture down the center of the prepared pan. Use the spatula to clean out the saucepan. Spread the mixture evenly to the sides and the corners of the pan. Let the pan sit on the counter for several hours. Put it in the refrigerator for 15 minutes just before cutting. Cut it right in the pan or slip the whole panful out onto the cutting board. To make bars, cut in half lengthwise. Cut in half crosswise. Cut each of the 4 sections into 6 bars. Store in a container with a lid with waxed paper between the layers or wrap individually in the plastic wrap. Makes 24 bars.

Pictured on page 35.

Plate Courtesy Of: IKEA

1. Peanut Chew page 34
2. Peanut Butter Cups

Peanut Butter Cups

These have a yummy surprise inside.

1.	**Semisweet chocolate chips**	**1 cup**	**250 mL**
	Milk chocolate chips	**½ cup**	**125 mL**
	Grated paraffin wax, lightly packed	**4 tbsp.**	**60 mL**
2.	**Smooth peanut butter**	**½ cup**	**125 mL**
	Icing (confectioner's) sugar	**¾ cup**	**175 mL**
	Graham cracker crumbs	**2 tbsp.**	**30 mL**

You will need: measuring spoons, measuring cups, a heavy medium saucepan, 2 mixing spoons, a hot pad, small foil or paper baking cups, a small spoon or paint brush, a rubber spatula, a medium bowl and a sharp knife.

1. Combine both chocolate chips and the wax in the saucepan on lowest heat. Stir continually until they melt. Remove the saucepan to the hot pad. Divide into 2 equal portions. Return 1 portion to saucepan. Measure 2 tsp. (10 mL) of the chocolate mixture and place in the bottom of one baking cup. Use the back of the small spoon or the paint brush to push the chocolate up the sides of the baking cup about ¼ inch (0.5 cm). Repeat steps for each foil cup until you have used 1 portion of the chocolate mixture. Place the cups in the refrigerator until hard.

2. Combine the remaining 3 ingredients in the bowl. Mix well. Divide in half. Roll each half into a rope. Cut each rope into enough pieces so that the total equals the number of prepared baking cups. Press each piece to fit over the chocolate in the paper cup. Chill 10 minutes. Warm the remaining chip mixture. Spoon 2 tsp. (10 mL) over the top of each cup. Chill. Serve at room temperature. Makes 24 chocolates.

Pictured above.

Hermits

These cookies are soft, spicy and nutty. Remind Mom and Dad these are a healthy after-school snack.

1. Butter or hard margarine, softened (at room temperature) ½ cup — 125 mL

1. Butter or hard margarine, softened (at room temperature)	½ cup	125 mL
Brown sugar, packed	1½ cups	375 mL
Large eggs	3	3
Vanilla flavoring	1 tsp.	5 mL
2. All-purpose flour	2 cups	450 mL
Baking powder	1 tsp.	5 mL
Baking soda	½ tsp.	2 mL
Salt	½ tsp.	2 mL
Ground cinnamon	1 tsp.	5 mL
Ground nutmeg	½ tsp.	2 mL
Ground allspice	¼ tsp.	1 mL
3. Chopped dates	1 cup	250 mL
Raisins	1 cup	250 mL
Chopped walnuts	½ cup	125 mL

You will need: a large bowl, measuring spoons, measuring cups, an electric mixer, a mixing spoon, cookie sheets, oven mitts, a wire rack, a pancake lifter and waxed paper.

1. Turn the oven on to 375°C (190°C). Put the butter or margarine, brown sugar and 1 egg into the bowl. Beat on low speed to blend. Beat in the next 2 eggs 1 at a time on medium speed. Add the vanilla flavoring. Mix it in.

2. Add the next 7 ingredients to the bowl. Beat on the lowest speed just until moistened.

3. Add the dates, raisins and walnuts. Stir with the spoon to mix them evenly. Grease the cookie sheets. Drop by rounded tablespoonfuls onto the cookie sheets, about 2 inches (5 cm) apart. Bake on the center rack in the the oven for 7 to 10 minutes. Use the oven mitts to remove the cookie sheets to the wire rack. Let stand 2 minutes before removing the cookies to the waxed paper on the counter. Cool completely. Store in a container with a lid. Makes about 3 dozen cookies.

Ginger Crinkles

Although these start from balls on a cookie sheet, they end up a flat cookie with a crinkled top.

1.			
	Butter or hard margarine, softened (at room temperature)	1 cup	250 mL
	Granulated sugar	1½ cups	375 mL
	Large egg	1	1
	Dark corn syrup	2 tbsp.	30 mL
	Mild molasses	½ cup	125 mL
2.	All-purpose flour	3 cups	750 mL
	Baking soda	2 tsp.	10 mL
	Ground cinnamon	2 tsp.	10 mL
	Ground ginger	1 tsp.	5 mL
	Ground cloves	¼ tsp.	1 mL
	Salt	½ tsp.	2 mL
3.	Granulated sugar, for coating	¼ cup	50 mL

You will need: a large bowl, measuring spoons, measuring cups, an electric mixer, a rubber spatula, a mixing spoon, a cereal bowl, cookie sheets, oven mitts, a wire rack, a pancake lifter and waxed paper.

1. Turn the oven on to 375°F (190°C). Put the first 5 ingredients into the bowl. Beat on low speed until blended. Beat on medium speed until smooth. Scrape the batter off the beaters into the bowl using the rubber spatula.

2. Add the next 6 ingredients. Stir with the spoon until moistened. Roll into 1½ inch (3.5 cm) balls.

3. Put the remaining sugar into the cereal bowl. Roll the balls, 1 at a time, in the sugar to coat them. Arrange the balls on the ungreased cookie sheets, 2 inches (5 cm) apart. Bake on the center rack in the oven for 12 to 14 minutes. Use the oven mitts to remove the cookie sheets to the wire rack. Let stand for about 2 minutes before removing the cookies to the waxed paper on the counter. Cool completely. Store in a container with a lid. Makes 3½ dozen cookies.

Pictured on page 117 and on the front cover.

Sugar Cookies

Especially made for decorating. This recipe doubles easily.

1. Butter or hard margarine,   **6 tbsp.**   **100 mL**
     softened (at room temperature)

Granulated sugar	½ cup	125 mL
Large egg	1	1
Vanilla flavoring	½ tsp.	2 mL

2.

All-purpose flour	1¼ cups	300 mL
Baking powder	¾ tsp.	4 mL
Salt	¼ tsp.	1 mL
Cardamom (optional but good)	⅛ tsp.	0.5 mL

3. Granulated sugar, sprinkle

You will need: a small bowl, measuring spoons, measuring cups, an electric mixer, a rubber spatula, a rolling pin, cookie sheets, a cookie cutter, a pancake lifter, oven mitts, a wire rack and waxed paper.

1. Put the first 4 ingredients into the bowl. Beat on medium speed until smooth.

2. Add the flour, baking powder, salt and cardamom. Beat on the lowest speed just until moistened. Cover the dough and chill in the refrigerator for 2 hours or overnight. Turn the oven on to 350°F (175°C). Grease the cookie sheets. Remove the dough from the refrigerator. Roll the dough, a handful at a time, on a lightly floured surface to about ⅛ inch (3 mm) thick. Use your favorite cookie cutters to cut out shapes. Arrange the cut out cookies on the cookie sheets.

3. Sprinkle the cookies with the sugar unless you plan to glaze or decorate. Bake on the center rack in the oven for about 10 minutes. Use the oven mitts to remove the cookie sheets to the wire rack. Let stand 2 minutes. Remove the cookies to the waxed paper on the counter. Cool completely. Decorate if you like. Store in a container with a lid. Makes about 3 dozen cookies.

Pictured on the front cover.

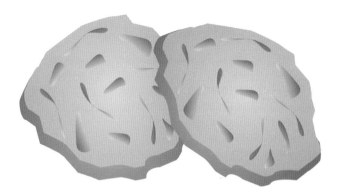

Butterscotch Oat Drops

A full-of-flavor, chewy cookie. Easy to double the recipe.

1. Butter or hard margarine,   ½ cup   125 mL
    softened (at room temperature)

Brown sugar, packed	½ cup	125 mL
Granulated sugar	¼ cup	50 mL
Large egg	1	1
Vanilla flavoring	½ tsp.	2 mL

2.
All-purpose flour	1 cup	250 mL
Rolled oats	1 cup	200 mL
Baking powder	½ tsp.	2 mL
Baking soda	½ tsp.	2 mL
Salt	½ tsp.	2 mL

You will need: measuring spoons, measuring cups, a medium bowl, an electric mixer, cookie sheets, a mixing spoon, oven mitts, a wire rack, a pancake lifter and waxed paper.

1. Turn the oven on to 350°F (175°C). Place the butter or margarine in the bowl. Add both sugars, egg and vanilla flavoring. Beat on medium speed until smooth.

2. Add the rest of the ingredients to the batter in the bowl. Stir with the spoon just until moistened. Drop by rounded teaspoonfuls onto the ungreased cookie sheets. Leave 2 inches (5 cm) between each mound of dough. Bake on the center rack in the oven for 8 to 10 minutes. Use the oven mitts to remove the cookie sheet to the wire rack. Let stand 2 minutes before removing the cookies to the waxed paper on the counter. Cool completely. Store the cookies in a container with a lid. Makes about 3 dozen cookies.

Peanut Butter Gems

One of your favorite cookies—with faces!

1. Butter or hard margarine,   ½ cup   125 mL
    softened (at room temperature)
    Brown sugar, packed   ⅔ cup   150 mL
    Granulated sugar   ⅓ cup   75 mL
    Large egg   1   1
    Smooth peanut butter   ½ cup   125 mL
    Vanilla flavoring   1 tsp.   5 mL

2. All-purpose flour   1½ cups   375 mL
    Baking soda   1 tsp.   5 mL
    Salt   ⅛ tsp.   0.5 mL

3. Candy coated chocolate bits,
    such as Smarties or M & M's

You will need: cookie sheets, a medium bowl, measuring spoons, measuring cups, an electric mixer, a rubber spatula, a mixing spoon, a table fork, oven mitts, a wire rack, a pancake lifter and waxed paper.

1. Turn the oven on to 350°F (175°C). Grease the cookie sheets. Combine the first 6 ingredients in the bowl. Beat on low speed until everything is moistened. Beat on medium speed until smooth. Scrape the batter off the beaters into the bowl using the rubber spatula.

2. Add the flour, baking soda and salt. Stir with the spoon to moisten. Using the palms of your hands, roll the dough into 1½ inch (3.5 cm) balls. Arrange the balls on the cookie sheets, about 2 inches (5 cm) apart. Press down with the fork or with your hand or the bottom of a glass. If sticky, dip the glass into some flour between presses.

3. Bake on the center rack in the oven for 10 to 12 minutes. Use the oven mitts to remove the cookie sheets to the wire rack. Let stand 2 minutes. Remove the cookies to the waxed paper on the counter. Cool completely. Store the cookies in a container with a lid. Makes 24 to 30 cookies.

Pictured on page 41 and on the front cover.

(continued on next page)

LOLLIPOPS: Use Peanut Butter Gems, page 40 or Sugar Cookies, page 38. Shape ¼ cup (50 mL) of the dough into a ball. Insert a wooden popsicle stick halfway into the dough. Press with the bottom of a glass or your hand to make it ⅜ inch (9 mm) thick. Bake in a 350°F (175°C) oven for 9 to 12 minutes. If you make them thicker, they will take a bit longer to cook. Use the oven mitts to remove the cookie sheets to the wire rack.

Decorate with icing or if you want to apply some decorations, warm some light corn syrup. Brush the tops of the lollipops with the warm syrup. This will make them sticky. Apply the decorations you choose.

Pictured below.

Jumbo Raisin Cookies

You can make these as jumbo as you like.

1.	Raisins	1 cup	250 mL
	Water	½ cup	125 mL
2.	Butter or hard margarine, softened (at room temperature)	½ cup	125 mL
	Granulated sugar	1 cup	250 mL
	Large eggs	2	2
	Vanilla flavoring	½ tsp.	2 mL
3.	All-purpose flour	2 cups	500 mL
	Salt	1 tsp.	5 mL
	Baking soda	½ tsp.	2 mL
	Ground cinnamon	¾ tsp.	4 mL
	Ground nutmeg	⅛ tsp.	0.5 mL
	Ground allspice	⅛ tsp.	0.5 mL
	Chopped walnuts	½ cup	125 mL

You will need: cookie sheets, a small saucepan, a hot pad, measuring cups, a mixing spoon, a large bowl, measuring spoons, an electric mixer, a rubber spatula, oven mitts, a wire rack, a pancake lifter and waxed paper.

1. Turn the oven on to 350°F (175°C). Grease the cookie sheets. Combine the raisins and water in the small saucepan. Stir. Heat on medium until it boils. Boil slowly for 5 minutes. Remove the saucepan to the hot pad. Cool.

2. Put the butter or margarine into the bowl. Add the sugar, eggs and vanilla flavoring. Beat on low speed to mix, then beat on medium speed until smooth. Scrape the batter off the beaters into the bowl using the rubber spatula. Add the raisins and water to the batter. Stir with the spoon to mix.

3. Add the rest of the ingredients. Stir until mixed. Drop by rounded tablespoonfuls onto the cookie sheets, about 2 inches (5 cm) apart. Bake on the center rack in the oven for 12 to 15 minutes. Use the oven mitts to remove the cookie sheets to the wire rack. Let stand 2 minutes. Remove the cookies to the waxed paper on the counter. Cool completely.
Store the cookies in a container with a lid.
Makes about 30 cookies.

Chocolate Oat Chippers

A chewy lunchbox cookie.

1.
Butter or hard margarine, softened (at room temperature)	½ **cup**	125 mL
Brown sugar, packed	1 cup	250 mL
Large egg	1	1
Vanilla flavoring	½ **tsp.**	2 mL

2.
All-purpose flour	1 cup	250 mL
Quick rolled oats	1 cup	250 mL
Baking soda	½ **tsp.**	2 mL
Salt	¼ **tsp.**	1 mL
Semisweet chocolate chips	1 cup	250 mL
Chopped walnuts (optional)	½ **cup**	125 mL

You will need: a large bowl, measuring spoons, measuring cups, a mixing spoon, an electric mixer, cookie sheets, oven mitts, a wire rack, a pancake lifter, and waxed paper.

1. Turn the oven on to 350°F (175°C). Put the butter or margarine into the bowl. Add the brown sugar, egg and vanilla flavoring. Beat on medium speed until smooth.

2. Add the rest of the ingredients. Stir with the spoon until all of the flour is mixed in. Grease the cookie sheets. Drop by rounded tablespoonfuls onto the cookie sheets, 2 inches (5 cm) apart. This will allow room for the cookies to spread out. Bake on the center rack in the oven for 10 to 12 minutes. Use the oven mitts to remove the cookie sheets to the wire rack. Let stand 2 minutes. Remove the cookies to the waxed paper on the counter. Cool completely. Store the cookies in a container with a lid with waxed paper between the layers. Makes about 3 dozen cookies.

Fruity S'Mores

New, improved S'mores with a fruit surprise. Make lots.

1.	**Large marshmallow**	**1**	**1**
2.	**Graham cracker squares**	**2**	**2**
	Squares of thin milk chocolate bar	**2-6**	**2-6**
	Thin slices of strawberry or halves of seedless grape	**2**	**2**

You will need: a long-handled toasting fork and a small plate.

1. Stick the fork in the end of the marshmallow, about ½ way through. Hold it over a fire or a very hot burner until it is toasty brown and soft.

2. Place one of the graham cracker squares on the plate. Place the chocolate on the square. Push the marshmallow on top of the chocolate. Place the fruit slices on top of the marshmallow. Top with the second cracker. Push down, holding a few moments so the chocolate begins to melt. Makes 1 treat.

Pictured below.

1. Fruity S'Mores
2. Fiddle Diddles page 45

Plate Courtesy Of:
The Bay China Dept.

Fiddle Diddles

A no-bake cookie that always turns out. Chocolate-flavored and nutty.

1.	**Butter or hard margarine**	**¹/₂ cup**	**125 mL**
	Granulated sugar	**2 cups**	**500 mL**
	Milk	**¹/₂ cup**	**125 mL**
2.	**Cocoa**	**6 tbsp.**	**100 mL**
	Quick cooking rolled oats	**3 cups**	**750 mL**
	(not instant)		
	Medium coconut	**¹/₂ cup**	**125 mL**
	Chopped walnuts	**¹/₂ cup**	**125 mL**
	Salt, just a pinch		
	Vanilla flavoring	**1 tsp.**	**5 mL**

You will need: a large saucepan, measuring cups, measuring spoons, a mixing spoon, a hot pad and waxed paper on a cookie sheet.

1. Put the butter or margarine, sugar and milk into the saucepan. Heat on medium, stirring often, until it comes to a boil. Remove the pan to the hot pad.

2. Add all of the remaining ingredients. Stir well. Drop by rounded teaspoonfuls onto the waxed paper. Cool completely. Store in a container with a lid with waxed paper between the layers. Makes about 40 cookies.

Pictured on page 44 and below.

Plate Courtesy Of:
The Bay China Dept.

Corn Flakes Stacks

Very tasty little morsels.

1.	McIntosh Toffee bars	3 × 2 oz.	3 × 56 g
	Butter or hard margarine	4 tbsp.	60 mL
	Milk	2 tbsp.	30 mL
2.	Corn flakes cereal	3 cups	750 mL

You will need: a table knife, a double boiler, measuring spoons, a mixing spoon , a hot pad, measuring cups and waxed paper on a cookie sheet.

1. Break up the toffee bars by placing one bar in the palm of your hand. Use the handle of the knife to hit it, cracking it. Put the toffee, butter or margarine and milk into the top of the double boiler. Put some hot water in the bottom of the double boiler. Set the top part in the bottom part and place over medium heat. Stir occasionally until the toffee mixture melts and is smooth. Remove the double boiler to the hot pad.

2. Add the corn flakes. Stir to coat well. Let the mixture stand for about 30 minutes until it hardens a bit but is still sticky. It makes it much easier to shape. Drop by rounded tablespoonfuls onto the waxed paper, shaping into mounds. Let stand on the counter for several hours or chill in the refrigerator for an hour if you want to eat them sooner. Store in a container with a lid with waxed paper between the layers. Makes 20 cookies.

Pictured above.

Butterscotch Sauce

So good over ice cream.

1.	Brown sugar, packed	1½ cups	375 mL
	All-purpose flour	1 tbsp.	15 mL
2.	Dark corn syrup	½ cup	125 mL
	Butter or hard margarine	2 tbsp.	30 mL
	Salt	⅛ tsp.	0.5 mL
	Evaporated milk	1 cup	250 mL

You will need: a medium saucepan, measuring spoons, measuring cups, a mixing spoon and a hot pad.

1. Put the sugar and flour into the saucepan. Stir well.

2. Add the rest of the ingredients to the saucepan. Heat and stir on medium until it starts to boil. Remove the saucepan to the hot pad. Cool. The sauce thickens when it cools. Store, covered, in the refrigerator. Makes 1⅞ cups (450 mL).

Pictured on page 59.

Hot Fudge Sauce

A necessity for ice cream, milk shakes, chocolate milk and hot chocolate.

1.	Cocoa	1 cup	250 mL
	Granulated sugar	1 cup	250 mL
	Water	1 cup	250 mL
	Vanilla flavoring	1 tsp.	5 mL
	Salt	¼ tsp.	1 mL

You will need: measuring spoons, measuring cups, a medium saucepan, a mixing spoon and a hot pad.

1. Combine all of the ingredients in the saucepan. Stir over medium heat until it boils. Boil slowly for 7 minutes, stirring occasionally. Remove the saucepan to the hot pad. Cool. The sauce thickens when it cools. Store, covered, in the refrigerator. Makes 1⅔ cups (400 mL).

Pictured on page 59.

Crispy Fruit Pizza

A dessert pizza you can eat with your fingers. Can be made the day before. This is AWESOME! Do not freeze.

1. CRUST		
Butter or hard margarine	¼ cup	60 mL
Large marshmallows	32	32
2. Crisp rice cereal	5 cups	1.25 L
3. TOPPING		
Cream cheese, softened (at room temperature)	8 oz.	250 g
Icing (confectioner's) sugar	2 cups	500 mL
Cocoa	¼ cup	60 mL
4. Small strawberries, halved, reserve 1 whole berry	16	16
Banana, peeled and sliced	1	1
Kiwifruit, peeled, halved lengthwise and sliced	2	2
5. GLAZE		
Apricot jam	2 tbsp.	30 mL
Water	1½ tsp.	7 mL
6. Whipping cream (or 1 envelope of topping)	1 cup	250 mL
Granulated sugar	2 tsp.	10 mL
Vanilla flavoring	½ tsp.	2 mL

You will need: a large saucepan, measuring cups, 3 mixing spoons, a hot pad, a 12 inch (30 cm) pizza pan, a small bowl, an electric mixer, measuring spoons, a small cup, a pastry brush and a medium bowl.

1. Crust: Combine the butter or margarine and marshmallows in the saucepan. Stir often on medium-low heat until melted.

2. Remove the saucepan to the hot pad. Add the rice cereal. Stir until it is well coated. Grease the pizza pan. Press the cereal mixture evenly over the pan with your wet fingers. Cool in the refrigerator.

3. Topping: Place the cream cheese, icing sugar and cocoa in the small bowl. Beat on low speed until moistened. Beat on medium speed until smooth. Spread over the cooled pizza base.

(continued on next page)

4. Arrange the strawberries, bananas and kiwifruit over the chocolate topping in a fancy design.

5. **Glaze:** Mix the jam and water in the cup. With the pastry brush, dab the fruit with the jam mixture to glaze and to prevent the fruit from turning brown.

6. Beat the whipping cream, sugar and vanilla flavoring in the medium bowl until thick. Put dabs on top of the pizza. Cuts into 8 or 10 wedges.

Pictured below.

Dirt Cake

A fun way to gross out your friends. Do not freeze.

1.	**Package of cream-filled chocolate cookies**	**1 lb.**	**454 g**
2.	**Butter or hard margarine, softened (at room temperature)**	**¼ cup**	**50 mL**
	Cream cheese, softened (at room temperature)	**8 oz.**	**250 g**
	Icing (confectioner's) sugar	**1 cup**	**250 mL**
	Vanilla flavoring	**1 tsp.**	**5 mL**
3.	**Instant chocolate puddings, 4 servings per box**	**4**	**4**
	Milk	**6 cups**	**1.35 L**
4.	**Frozen whipped topping, thawed**	**4⅓ cups**	**1 L**
5.	**Gummy worms**	**15**	**15**

You will need: a blender or food processor, measuring cups, a large bowl, measuring spoons, an electric beater, a large bowl, a rubber spatula, a 9 x 13 inch (22 x 33 cm) pan or a large flower pot or 2 smaller pots.

1. Put the cookies in the blender or food processor and process until they become fine crumbs. Set aside.

2. Put the butter or margarine, cream cheese, icing sugar and vanilla flavoring in the bowl . Beat on low speed to mix then beat on medium speed until smooth.

3. Add the chocolate pudding powders and milk to the bowl. Beat on low speed to combine.

4. Fold the whipped topping into the pudding mixture with the rubber spatula. Assemble in the ungreased pan or flower pot or pots in layers as follows:

> 1st layer: - ⅓ cookie crumbs
> 2nd layer: - ½ pudding mixture
> 3rd layer: - ⅓ cookie crumbs
> 4th layer: - ½ pudding mixture
> 5th layer: - ⅓ cookie crumbs

(continued on next page)

5. Tuck the ends of the gummy worms in the cookie "dirt". Be sure to have a worm on each piece. Store in the refrigerator. Chill for at least 3 hours before serving. Cuts into 15 squares, or serve with a clean garden trowel or a toy sand shovel if serving in the flowerpot.

Pictured below.

Pot Courtesy Of: IKEA

Dark Blue Heaven Dessert

This easy dessert looks as delicious as it tastes.

1.	Canned crushed pineapple, with juice	19 oz.	540 mL
	Canned blueberry pie filling	19 oz.	540 mL
	Yellow cake mix, 2 layer size	1	1
2.	Granulated sugar	1 tbsp.	15 mL
	Ground cinnamon	½ tsp.	2 mL
3.	Butter or hard margarine, thinly sliced	1 cup	250 mL
	Chopped walnuts	¾ cup	175 mL

You will need: a 9 x 13 inch (22 x 33 cm) pan, a small mixing spoon, a rubber spatula, measuring spoons, measuring cups, a small cup, oven mitts and a wire rack.

1. Turn the oven on to 350°F (175°C). Grease the pan. Spread the pineapple and juice in the pan. Put small spoonfuls of the pie filling here and there over the pineapple. Empty the can with the spatula. Sprinkle the dry cake mix evenly over the pie filling.

2. Mix the sugar and cinnamon in the small cup. Sprinkle over the cake mix.

3. Arrange the sliced butter or margarine over the top of the cake mix. Sprinkle with the walnuts. Bake on the center rack in the oven for 45 to 55 minutes. A wooden toothpick inserted in the center of the cake should come out clean. Use the oven mitts to remove the pan to the wire rack. Serve in squares, warm with ice cream, or cold with whipped cream or ice cream. Cuts into 15 pieces.

Pictured below.

Plate Courtesy Of:
Call The Kettle Black

Raisin Cobbler

If your favorite filling is blueberry or cherry, use it rather than the raisin. Good and easy.

1.	Raisin pie filling	19 oz.	540 mL
	Lemon juice, fresh or bottled	1 tsp.	5 mL
2.	Large egg	1	1
	Cooking oil	⅓ cup	75 mL
	Milk	⅓ cup	75 mL
3.	All-purpose flour	1½ cups	350 mL
	Granulated sugar	⅓ cup	75 mL
	Baking powder	2 tsp.	10 mL
	Salt	½ tsp.	2 mL

You will need: an 8 inch (20 cm) casserole dish, measuring spoons, 2 mixing spoons, a medium bowl, measuring cups, oven mitts and a wire rack.

1. Turn the oven on to 400°F (205°C). Pour the raisin pie filling into the ungreased casserole dish. Add the lemon juice. Stir into the filling. Place, uncovered, in the oven to heat while preparing the topping.

2. Break the egg into the bowl. Beat with the spoon until fairly smooth. Add the cooking oil and milk to the egg. Stir.

3. Add the flour, sugar, baking powder and salt. Stir just until moistened. Use the oven mitts to remove the casserole dish to the wire rack. Drop the batter by rounded tablespoonfuls over top of the filling. Return the casserole dish to the oven. Bake, uncovered, on the center rack in the oven for 20 to 25 minutes. A wooden toothpick inserted in the center of the topping should come out clean. Use the oven mitts to remove the casserole dish to the wire rack. Serve warm. Serves 6.

Pictured below.

Plate Courtesy Of:
Call The Kettle Black

Fudgesicles

A snap to make. The sugar may be cut in half with only a touch of flavor change.

1. Instant chocolate pudding,	1	1
4 servings per box		
Cold milk	$2\frac{1}{2}$ cups	625 mL
Granulated sugar	$\frac{1}{2}$ cup	125 mL

You will need: a small bowl, measuring cups, an electric mixer and fudgesicle molds.

1. Put all 3 ingredients into the bowl. Beat on slow speed until creamy thick. Pour into fudgesicle molds. Freeze for about 8 hours or overnight. Makes 3 cups (750 mL) or about 12 molds.

Variation: A 6 serving size regular chocolate pudding may be cooked with $3\frac{3}{4}$ cups (925 mL) milk. Stir in $\frac{1}{2}$ cup (125 mL) granulated sugar. Cool, stirring often. Pour into the molds.

Popsicles

You will eat these on hot days — and on cold days, too!

1.	**Orange-flavored gelatin (jelly powder)**	**3 oz.**	**85 g**
	Envelope of orange Kool-Aid drink mix or Freshie, without sugar	**1 × ¼ oz.**	**1 × 6 g**
	Granulated sugar	**1 cup**	**250 mL**
	Boiling water	**2 cups**	**500 mL**
2.	**Cold water**	**2½ cups**	**625 mL**

You will need: a medium bowl, a tea kettle, a mixing spoon, measuring cups, a pitcher and popsicle molds.

1. Combine the flavored gelatin, Kool-Aid and sugar in the bowl. Pour the boiling water over the top. Stir until everything is dissolved.

2. Add the cold water to the bowl. Stir. Use the pitcher or cup with a pouring spout to fill popsicle molds. Freeze for about 8 hours or overnight. Makes a generous 4 cups (1 L), enough for about 16 popsicles.

Variations: Use lime-flavored gelatin (jelly powder) with lime drink mix, lemon-flavored gelatin (jelly powder) with lemon drink mix, grape-flavored gelatin (jelly powder) with grape drink mix, strawberry-flavored gelatin (jelly powder) with strawberry drink mix.

HOT DAY TREAT: Freeze your favorite soft drink in an ice cube tray. Place several frozen cubes in a glass and enjoy them as long they last.

Butterscotch Freezies

A yummy treat.

1.	**Instant butterscotch pudding and pie filling, 4 serving size**	1	1
	Milk	2 cups	500 mL
2.	**Chopped walnuts or pecans (optional)**	⅓ cup	75 mL

You will need: a medium bowl, measuring cups, a mixing spoon, and popsicle or fudgesicle molds.

1. Stir the pudding mix and milk together in the bowl until blended.

2. Add the walnuts or pecans. Stir. Pour or spoon into the molds. Makes 2 cups (500 mL), enough for 8 popsicles or fudgesicles. Freeze for about 8 hours or overnight.

Creamy Popsicles

Make any flavor you want. Just combine the same flavor of gelatin as yogurt. A good cooler.

1. **Strawberry or raspberry-flavored** **gelatin (jelly powder)**	**3 oz.**	**85 g**
Boiling water	**1 cup**	**250 mL**
2. **Strawberry or raspberry yogurt**	**1 cup**	**250 mL**
Cold water	**½ cup**	**125 mL**

You will need: a medium bowl, a tea kettle, measuring cups, a mixing spoon and popsicle molds.

1. Pour the flavored gelatin into the bowl. Add the boiling water. Stir thoroughly until the gelatin is dissolved.

2. Add the yogurt to the gelatin mixture. Stir well. Add the cold water. Stir. Pour into the molds. Freeze for about 8 hours or overnight. Makes 2⅔ cups (650 mL), about 10 or 11 popsicles.

Banana Split

So colorful. This is equally delicious using just vanilla ice cream. Do not freeze. Pictured on page 59.

1.			
Banana, peeled and cut lengthwise	1	1
Vanilla ice cream scoop	1	1
Strawberry ice cream scoop	1	1
Chocolate ice cream scoop	1	1

2. TOPPING			
Butterscotch sauce, page 47	1-2 tbsp.	15-30 mL
Strawberry jam	1-2 tbsp.	15-30 mL
Chocolate syrup	1-2 tbsp.	15-30 mL
Maraschino cherry		
Candied sprinkles		
Whipped cream or topping		

You will need: a banana split dish or soup bowl, an ice cream scoop and measuring spoons.

1. Lay the banana halves in the banana split dish. Arrange the scoops of ice cream down the center between the banana halves.

2. Topping: Put 1 or 2 spoonfuls of sauce over top of the ice cream scoops (chocolate sauce over the chocolate ice cream, strawberry sauce over the strawberry ice cream and the butterscotch sauce over the vanilla ice cream). Sprinkle with candied sprinkles and any other toppings you like such as: miniature marshmallows, orange segments, chopped nuts, candy-coated chocolate, whipped cream or crushed cookies. Serves 1.

Hot Fudge Sundae

Simply an irresistible concoction. Pictured on page 59.

1.			
Large scoop of vanilla ice cream, or 2 smaller scoops	1	1
Hot fudge sauce, page 47	2 tbsp.	30 mL
Chopped peanuts or other nuts (optional)	1 tbsp.	15 mL

You will need: a cereal bowl or glass dish, an ice cream scoop and measuring spoons.

1. Place a large scoop of ice cream in the bowl. Spoon hot fudge sauce over the ice cream. Sprinkle with nuts. Serves 1.

1. Hot Fudge Sauce page 47
2. Hot Fudge Sundae page 58
3. Chocolate Syrup
4. Strawberry Jam
5. Butterscotch Sauce page 47
6. Banana Split page 58

Pebble Ice Cream Dish Courtesy Of:
Le Gnome
Ice Cream Boat Dish Courtesy Of:
Mugsie's Coffee House

Pork Chops

Chops are cooked with a dark sauce.

1.	Cooking oil	1 tbsp.	15 mL
	Pork chops, trimmed of fat	6	6
2.	Peeled and chopped onion	1 cup	250 mL
3.	Ketchup	½ cup	125 mL
	Brown sugar, packed	¼ cup	50 mL
	White vinegar	3 tbsp.	45 mL
	Soy sauce	1 tbsp.	15 mL
	Salt	½ tsp.	2 mL
	Pepper	⅛ tsp.	0.5 mL

You will need: a frying pan, measuring spoons, a table fork, a small roaster, measuring cups, a small bowl, a mixing spoon, oven mitts and a hot pad.

1. Turn the oven on to 350°F (175°C). Put the cooking oil in the frying pan and heat to medium. Place the pork chops in the frying pan. Brown on both sides. Transfer the chops to the roaster.

2. Scatter the onion over the chops in the roaster.

3. Measure all of the remaining ingredients into the bowl. Stir. Pour over the chops and onions. Cover the roaster with the lid. Bake on the center rack in the oven for about 1 hour until the meat is tender. Use the oven mitts to remove the roaster to the hot pad. Makes 6 small servings.

Pictured below.

Plate Courtesy Of:
The Bay China Dept.

Salmon Casserole

Nothing could be easier and quicker to prepare. A good light lunch dish.

1.			
	Canned salmon, drained	2 x 7½ oz.	2 x 213 g
	Dry bread crumbs	1 cup	250 mL
2.	SAUCE		
	Butter or hard margarine	6 tbsp.	100 mL
	All-purpose flour	6 tbsp.	100 mL
	Salt	¾ tsp.	4 mL
	Pepper	¼ tsp.	1 mL
	Milk	3⅓ cups	825 mL

You will need: a table fork, an 8 inch (20 cm) casserole dish, measuring cups, a medium saucepan, measuring spoons, a mixing spoon, a table knife, oven mitts and a hot pad.

1. Turn the oven on to 350°F (175°C). Remove the skin and round bones from the salmon with the fork. Crumble ½ of the salmon into the ungreased casserole dish. Sprinkle ½ of the crumbs over top.

2. Sauce: Melt the butter or margarine in the saucepan over medium heat. Mix in the flour, salt and pepper. Stir in the milk until it comes to a boil. Stir continually so it doesn't go lumpy. A whisk works really well for avoiding lumps. Pour ⅓ of the sauce over the crumbs in the casserole. Crumble the second ½ of the salmon over top, followed by the second ½ of the crumbs. Pour the remaining sauce over the top layer of crumbs. Use the knife to poke holes here and there to allow a bit of the sauce to sink in. Bake, uncovered, on the center rack in the oven for about 30 minutes until hot and bubbly. Use the oven mitts to remove the casserole dish to the hot pad. Serves 6.

Pictured below.

Casserole Dish Courtesy Of:
The Enchanted Kitchen

Spaghetti Dish

Cook this on the top of the stove all in one pot. This has a wonderful tomato flavor.

1.	Cooking oil	1 tbsp.	15 mL
	Lean ground beef	1 lb.	454 g
	Peeled and chopped onion	1 cup	250 mL
2.	Canned tomatoes, broken up, with juice	14 oz.	398 mL
	Canned sliced mushrooms, with juice	10 oz.	284 mL
	Tomato paste	5½ oz.	156 mL
	Water	1½ cups	375 mL
	Garlic powder	¼ tsp.	1 mL
	Dried basil	¼ tsp.	1 mL
	Dried oregano	¼ tsp.	1 mL
	Parsley flakes	1 tsp.	5 mL
	Granulated sugar	1 tsp.	5 mL
	Grated Parmesan cheese	¼ cup	50 mL
	Salt	1½ tsp.	7 mL
	Pepper	¼ tsp.	1 mL
	Bay leaf	1	1
3.	Spaghetti, broken, uncooked	8 oz.	250 g
4.	Grated Parmesan cheese, sprinkle		

You will need: An extra large saucepan or Dutch oven, measuring spoons, measuring cups, a large mixing spoon and a hot pad.

1. Heat the cooking oil in the saucepan on medium. Add the ground beef and onion. Scramble-fry until browned and crumbly looking.

2. Add the next 13 ingredients to the saucepan. Stir well.

3. Add the spaghetti. Make sure all of the spaghetti is covered with some of the sauce. Cover with the lid. Bring to a boil. Reduce the heat so it boils gently for 11 to 13 minutes until the spaghetti is tender but firm. Remove the saucepan to the hot pad. Throw away the bay leaf.

4. Sprinkle with the Parmesan cheese. Makes 7⅔ cups (1.75 L). Serves 4.

Pictured on page 63.

Spaghetti Dish page 62

Bowl Courtesy Of:
The Bay Housewares Dept.

Oven Roasted Meal

When it's your turn to prepare supper, this is a snap. And it's so special.

1. Beef roast, boneless, eye of round, sirloin tip or rump roast, size can be a bit more or less	2¼ lbs.	1 kg
2. Hot water	½ cup	125 mL
Beef bouillon powder	½ tsp.	2 mL
3. Medium potatoes, peeled and halved crosswise	6	6
Medium carrots, peeled and halved crosswise, cut large end in half lengthwise	6	6
Medium parsnips, peeled and cut like carrots	4	4
Medium onions, peeled and quartered	2	2

You will need: a medium roaster, measuring spoons, measuring cups, a small cup, a small mixing spoon, oven mitts, a hot pad, a platter and aluminum foil.

1. Turn the oven on to 300°F (150°C). Place the roast in the middle of the roaster.

2. Stir the water with the beef bouillon powder in the cup. Pour over the roast.

3. Arrange the prepared vegetables around the roast. Cover with the roaster lid. Bake on the center rack in the oven for about 2 hours until the meat is tender and the vegetables are cooked. Use the oven mitts to remove the roaster to the hot pad. Place the roast on the platter and cover with the foil while you make the gravy. Serves 4 to 6.

GRAVY: Pour the juice from the roaster into a measuring cup and then into a small saucepan. If you have 1 cup (250 mL) of juice, stir 1 tbsp. (15 mL) cornstarch into 2 tbsp. (30 mL) of water in a small cup. If you have 1½ cups (375 mL) of juice, use 1½ tbsp. (25 mL) of cornstarch. A bit of water can be added to bring the juice level up a touch more if it is a bit short. Pour into the juice. Heat and stir until it boils. Add a sprinkle of salt. Taste to see if you need to add more. Makes 1 to 1½ cups.

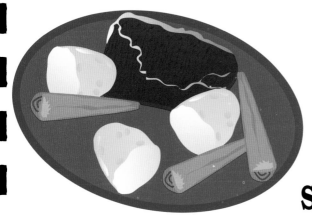

Sauced Wieners

This is ideal to serve over rice. It is good with potatoes or noodles, too.

1. **Canned unsweetened pineapple tidbits, with juice**	**14 oz.**	**398 mL**
Water	**1 cup**	**250 mL**
Soy sauce	**2 tbsp.**	**30 mL**
White vinegar	**¼ cup**	**50 mL**
Brown sugar, packed	**⅓ cup**	**75 mL**
Wieners, cut in 6-7 pieces each	**1 lb.**	**454 g**
2. **Cornstarch**	**¼ cup**	**50 mL**
Water	**⅓ cup**	**75 mL**

You will need: a medium saucepan, measuring spoons, measuring cups, a mixing spoon, a small cup, a small mixing spoon and a hot pad.

1. Combine the first 6 ingredients in the saucepan. Bring to a boil on medium heat, stirring often.

2. Mix the cornstarch and the last amount of the water in the small cup. Stir it into the boiling mixture until it returns to a boil and thickens. Remove the saucepan to the hot pad. Makes 6 servings.

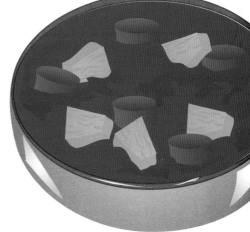

Macaroni Magic

Begin with a package and dress it up.

1.	Packaged macaroni and cheese dinner	7½ oz.	200 g
	Peeled and chopped onion	¾ cup	175 mL
2.	Canned sliced mushrooms, drained	10 oz.	284 mL
	Canned chicken flakes	6.5 oz.	184 g
3.	Large tomato, seeded and chopped	1	1
	Dried basil	1 tsp.	5 mL
	Granulated sugar	¼ tsp.	1 mL
	Salt, light sprinkle		
	Pepper, light sprinkle		

(continued on next page)

1. Macaroni Magic
2. Bologna Cups page 67

You will need: a large saucepan, measuring cups, a mixing spoon, an 8 inch (20 cm) casserole dish, a sharp knife, a small spoon, a small bowl, measuring spoons, oven mitts and a wire rack.

1. Turn the oven on to 350°F (175°C). Prepare the macaroni and cheese in the saucepan as the package directs. Add the onion to the macaroni before cooking.

2. Stir the mushrooms and chicken flakes into the prepared macaroni. Turn into the casserole dish.

3. Cut the tomato in half. Squeeze each tomato half to remove the juice and the seeds. Use the small spoon to help remove the rest of the seeds. Throw away the juice and seeds. Chop the tomato and place it in the bowl. Add the basil and sugar. Stir lightly. Sprinkle with the salt and pepper. Stir lightly once more. Pile on the top center of the casserole. Cover. Bake on the center rack in the oven for 20 to 30 minutes until heated through. Use the oven mitts to remove the casserole dish to the wire rack. Serves 4.

Pictured on page 66 and on the front cover.

Bologna Cups

Fill with Macaroni Magic, page 66, Scrambled Eggs, page 89, or any filling of your choice.

1. **Bologna slices**   4   4

You will need: a frying pan and a table fork.

1. Fry the slices of bologna in the frying pan for about 2 minutes. They will puff up in the center. Turn the slices over with the fork. Fry for about 1 minute more. Do not flatten. Remove and turn the cups right side up. Serves 4.

Pictured on page 66.

Stroganoff

Add a salad and a vegetable and you're all set. The pasta is added raw.

1.	Cooking oil	1 tbsp.	15 mL
	Lean ground beef	1 lb.	454 g
2.	Condensed cream of mushroom soup	10 oz.	284 mL
	Water	1 cup	250 mL
	Envelope of dry onion soup mix	1 × 1½ oz.	1 × 42 g
	Noodles, wide or medium, uncooked	1 cup	250 mL
	Canned sliced mushrooms, drained	10 oz.	284 mL
	Ketchup	1 tbsp.	15 mL
3.	Sour cream	½ cup	125 mL
	Yellow cheese slice, broken up	1	1

You will need: a frying pan with a lid, measuring spoons, a mixing spoon and measuring cups.

1. Heat the cooking oil in the frying pan. Add the ground beef. Scramble-fry until browned and crumbly looking.

2. Add the next 6 ingredients to the beef. Stir. Cover. Simmer on low heat for about 10 minutes until the pasta is tender but firm. Remove the lid.

3. Add the sour cream and cheese. Stir until the cheese melts. Serves 4 to 6.

Pictured below.

Bowl Courtesy Of:
IKEA

Snappy Lunch

An exceptionally good quick meal.

1.	**Canned kidney beans**	½ × **14 oz.**	½ × **398 mL**
	Salsa, mild or hot	**3 tbsp.**	**45 mL**
2.	**Grated mild or medium Cheddar cheese**	**2 tbsp.**	**30 mL**
	Grated Mozzarella cheese	**2 tbsp.**	**30 mL**
3.	**Crackers, cheese bun, bread slice**		

You will need: a small spoon, a cereal bowl, measuring spoons, oven mitts and a hot pad.

1. Spoon the ½ can of kidney beans into the bowl. Add the salsa. Stir together.

2. Sprinkle with both the cheeses. Heat in the microwave oven on High for about 2 minutes or until the cheese is melted. Use the oven mitts to remove the bowl to the hot pad. This may be eaten as is or it may be stirred first.

3. Eat with crackers, cheese bun or bread slice. Serves 1.

Pictured below.

Soup Bowl, Plate And Spoon Courtesy Of:
IKEA

Pizza

With a quickbread crust, this can be ready in short order.

1.	Biscuit mix	2 cups	500 mL
	Milk	½ cup	125 mL
2.	Tomato sauce	7½ oz.	213 mL
	Dried oregano	¾ tsp.	4 mL
	Dried basil	½ tsp.	2 mL
	Salt	½ tsp.	2 mL
3.	Cooking oil	1 tbsp.	15 mL
	Peeled and chopped onion	½ cup	125 mL
	Seeded and chopped green pepper	¼ cup	50 mL
4.	Smoked sausage, pepperoni, or summer sausage, sliced in ¼ inch (1 cm) slices	½ lb.	225 g
	Canned sliced mushrooms, drained (use part or all)	10 oz.	284 mL
	Sliced green or black olives, (optional)	10-12	10-12
	Grated mozzarella cheese	2 cups	500 mL
	Grated Parmesan cheese	2 tbsp.	30 mL

You will need: a 12 inch (30 cm) pizza pan, measuring cups, a medium bowl, a table fork, measuring spoons, a small bowl, a mixing spoon, a frying pan, oven mitts and a wire rack.

1. Turn the oven on to 400°F (205°C). Grease the pizza pan. Place the biscuit mix and milk into the medium bowl. Stir with the fork to form a ball. Knead the dough in the bowl 8 times. If the dough is sticky, knead in 1 or 2 tbsp. (15 or 30 mL) of flour. Press the dough over the bottom of the pizza pan.

2. Combine the tomato sauce, oregano, basil and salt in the small bowl. Stir. Set aside.

3. Heat the cooking oil in the frying pan. Add the onion and green pepper. Cook on medium until lightly browned. Add this mixture to the tomato sauce in the small bowl. Stir. Spread over the crust.

4. Sprinkle the sliced sausage over the tomato sauce mixture followed by the sliced mushrooms and the olives. Top with the mozzarella cheese. Sprinkle with the Parmesan cheese. Bake on the bottom rack in the oven for about 20 minutes. Use the oven mitts to remove the pizza pan to the wire rack. Let stand 5 minutes before cutting. Cuts into 8 wedges.

Tacos

A very different taco. Most enjoyable. Pictured above. Do not freeze.

1. **Frozen breaded fish sticks**   2   2

2. **Taco sauce (or seafood sauce)**   1 tbsp.   15 mL
    Chopped lettuce   ¼ cup   50 mL
    Tomato slice, diced   1   1
    Grated medium Cheddar cheese 2 tbsp. 30 mL
    Sour cream (optional)   1 tbsp.   15 mL

3. **Taco shells**   2   2

You will need: a frying pan, measuring spoons and measuring cups.

1. Heat the fish sticks in the frying pan or according to the package directions.

2. Prepare the next 5 ingredients. Set aside in separate dishes until ready to use as toppings for the tacos.

3. Put a fish stick in each taco shell. Divide and add in layers the taco sauce, lettuce, tomato, cheese and sour cream. Makes 2 tacos.

Chili

This chili contains canned beans in tomato sauce. Serve it in a bowl or spoon it over buns.

1.			
Cooking oil	1 tbsp.	15 mL
Lean ground beef	1 lb.	454 g
Peeled and chopped onion	1 cup	250 mL
Diced celery	$\frac{1}{3}$ cup	75 mL

2.		
Canned pork and beans or beans in tomato sauce (or kidney beans)	2 x 14 oz.	2 x 398 mL
Canned tomatoes, broken up, with juice	14 oz.	398 mL
Brown sugar, packed	$\frac{1}{4}$ cup	50 mL
Chili powder (add more if you like)	1 tsp.	5 mL
Beef bouillon powder	1 tsp.	5 mL
Salt	1 tsp.	5 mL
Pepper	$\frac{1}{4}$ tsp.	1 mL

You will need: a frying pan, measuring spoons, measuring cups, a mixing spoon and a large saucepan.

1. Heat the cooking oil in the frying pan. Add the ground beef, onion and celery. Scramble-fry until browned and crumbly looking. Turn into the saucepan.

2. Add all of the remaining ingredients to the saucepan. Stir. Heat on medium, stirring often until it comes to a boil. Turn the heat down so the chili simmers for 10 to 20 minutes, stirring often. Makes $6\frac{2}{3}$ cups (1.6 L).

Variation: Serve in a hollowed-out pumpkin, if desired.

Chicken Pasta Casserole

Make this the night before. Then all you have to do is put it in the oven the next day. The pasta is not precooked.

1.

Condensed cream of mushroom soup	10 oz.	284 mL
Condensed cream of celery soup	10 oz.	284 mL
Water	2½ cups	625 mL
Grated medium Cheddar cheese	2 cups	500 mL
Diced cooked chicken (see Note)	2 cups	500 mL
Macaroni, uncooked	2 cups	500 mL
Peeled and diced onion	1 cup	250 mL
Salt	1 tsp.	5 mL

2. Shoe string potato chips   1 cup   250 mL

You will need: a large bowl, measuring spoons, measuring cups, a 3 quart (3 L) casserole dish, a mixing spoon, oven mitts and a wire rack.

1. Mix the first 8 ingredients in the bowl. Turn into the ungreased casserole dish. Cover. Place in the refrigerator and leave overnight.

2. Turn the oven on to 350°F (175°C). Take the casserole dish from the refrigerator and remove the lid. Sprinkle the potato chips over the top. Use a few extra if you like. Bake, uncovered, on the center rack in the oven for 1 hour or until the pasta is tender. Use the oven mitts to remove the casserole dish to the wire rack. Serves 6 to 8.

Note: If you don't have cooked chicken on hand, use two 6.5 oz. (184 g) cans of flaked or chunk chicken, drained.

Pictured below.

Casserole Dish Courtesy Of:
Selfridge Pottery Studio

Dish Courtesy Of:
Reed's China And Gift Shop

Little Meat Muffins

Ten of the juiciest meat servings ever. Just the right size to freeze. They are thin enough to thaw quickly.

1. **Lean ground beef**	**1 lb.**	**454 g**
Condensed vegetable soup	**10 oz.**	**284 mL**

You will need: a medium bowl, a mixing spoon, a muffin pan, oven mitts and a wire rack.

1. Turn the oven on to 350°F (175°C). Mix the ground beef and soup in the bowl. Pack the beef mixture into 10 greased muffin cups. Bake on the center rack in the oven for about 40 to 45 minutes. Use the oven mitts to remove the muffin pan to the wire rack. Let stand 10 minutes before serving. Makes 10 meat muffins.

Pictured above.

Topsy Turvy Pizza

A very different method. The meat is cooked in the crust. The crust is soft enough to cut with a fork.

1. Cooking oil — 2 tsp. — 10 mL
Lean ground beef — ½ lb. — 227 g
Peeled and chopped onion — ½ cup — 125 mL

2. Large eggs — 3 — 3
Milk — ⅔ cup — 150 mL
All-purpose flour — 1 cup — 250 mL

3. Tomato sauce — 7½ oz. — 213 mL
Parsley flakes — 1 tsp. — 5 mL
Seasoned salt — 1 tsp. — 5 mL
Dried oregano — ¼ tsp. — 1 mL

4. Grated medium Cheddar cheese — 1 cup — 250 mL
Sliced fresh mushrooms — 1 cup — 250 mL
Sliced green pepper (or red pepper or both), seeds removed — ½ — ½
Grated mozzarella cheese — 1 cup — 250 mL

(continued on next page)

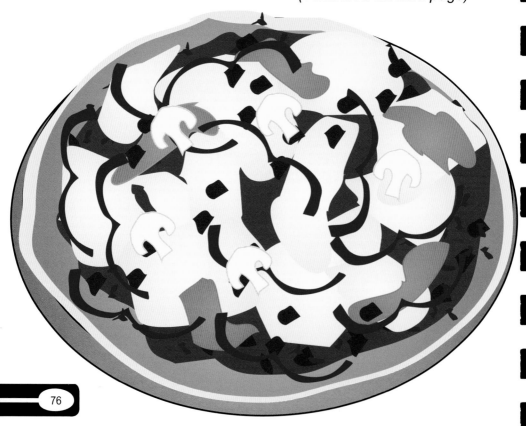

You will need: a frying pan, measuring spoons, measuring cups, 2 mixing spoons, a medium bowl, an electric mixer, a 12 inch (30 cm) pizza pan, a rubber spatula, oven mitts, a wire rack and a small bowl.

1. Turn the oven on to 425°F (220°C). Heat the cooking oil in the frying pan. Add the ground beef and onion. Scramble-fry until browned and crumbly looking.

2. Place the eggs, milk and flour in the medium bowl. Beat on medium speed until smooth. Grease the pizza pan. Pour the batter onto the pan and smooth with the spatula. Spoon the meat mixture evenly over top. Carefully put the pan on the bottom rack in the oven. Bake for about 20 minutes. Use the oven mitts to remove the pan to the wire rack.

3. Put the tomato sauce, parsley flakes, salt and oregano into the small bowl. Stir well. Pour and smooth over the pizza.

4. Sprinkle with the Cheddar cheese, then the mushrooms, green pepper and mozzarella cheese. Return the pizza to the oven for about 10 minutes more until bubbly and the cheese is melted. Use the oven mitts to remove the pizza pan to the wire rack. Let stand 5 minutes before cutting. Cuts into 8 wedges.

Caesar Salad

Almost like the adult version but so quick and easy. Make it for the whole family. Do not freeze.

1. **DRESSING**

White vinegar	2 tbsp.	30 mL
Water	2 tbsp.	30 mL
Cooking oil	2 tsp.	10 mL
Granulated sugar	2 tsp.	10 mL
Prepared mustard	½ tsp.	2 mL
Garlic powder	¼ tsp.	1 mL

2.

Head of Romaine lettuce	1	1
Croutons	1½ cups	375 mL
Grated Parmesan cheese	½ cup	125 mL
Hard-boiled eggs, (see page 81), peeled and chopped	2	2

You will need: measuring spoons, measuring cups, a small bowl, a mixing spoon, plastic wrap, a sharp knife, a large bowl and a pair of salad tongs or 2 spoons.

1. **Dressing:** Combine the first 6 ingredients in the small bowl. Stir well. Cover with plastic wrap and chill in the refrigerator until you're ready to toss the salad.

2. Wash and dry the lettuce. Tear or cut into bite-size pieces. Put the lettuce into the large bowl. Add the croutons, cheese and eggs. Cover with plastic wrap and put in the refrigerator. Just before serving, pour the dressing over the lettuce mixture. Use the salad tongs to toss and coat the lettuce with the dressing. Serves 6 to 8.

Pictured below.

Plate Courtesy Of:
Chintz & Company

Taco Salad

Serve with hamburgers or on its own as a meal. Do not freeze.

1. Head lettuce, cut in bite size pieces (about ½ medium head)	4 cups	1 L
Grated medium Cheddar cheese	1 cup	250 mL
Canned kidney beans, drained	14 oz.	398 mL
Large tomato, halved	1	1
Sliced green onions	4	4
2. Tortilla chips, broken up	8 oz.	225 g
3. Salad dressing (or mayonnaise)	½ cup	125 mL
Envelope taco seasoning mix (use ½ envelope)	½ x 1¼ oz.	½ x 35 g

You will need: measuring cups, a large bowl, a small spoon, a sharp knife, plastic wrap, a small bowl, a small mixing spoon and a pair of salad tongs or 2 spoons.

1. Put the lettuce, cheese and kidney beans into the large bowl. Squeeze each tomato half to remove the juice and the seeds. Use the small spoon to help remove the rest of the seeds. Throw away the juice and seeds. Dice the tomato. Add the tomato and onion to the lettuce mixture. Cover with plastic wrap and chill in the refrigerator until ready to serve.

2. Just before you plan to serve this salad, add the tortilla chips. If added too soon they will get soggy.

3. Stir the salad dressing and the taco seasoning together in the small bowl. Pour over the salad. Use the salad tongs to toss and coat the lettuce mixture with the dressing. Makes 8 side salads.

Pictured below.

Plate Courtesy Of:
Chintz & Company

Carrot Raisin Salad

For kids of all ages. Tasty. Do not freeze.

1.	**Peeled carrots**	**2-3**	**2-3**
	Raisins	**½ cup**	**125 mL**
	Canned crushed pineapple, drained	**½ cup**	**125 mL**
2.	**Salad dressing (or mayonnaise)**	**⅓ cup**	**75 mL**
	White vinegar	**2 tsp.**	**10 mL**
	Granulated sugar	**2 tsp.**	**10 mL**

You will need: a fine grater, measuring cups, a medium bowl, a mixing spoon, measuring spoons and a small bowl.

1. Use the grater to grate the carrots. You should have 2 cups (500 mL). Combine the carrots, raisins and pineapple in the medium bowl. Stir.

2. Put the salad dressing, vinegar and sugar into the small bowl. Mix well. Pour over the carrot mixture. Stir. Makes about 2 cups (500 mL).

Pictured above.

Hard-Boiled Eggs

A simple method for a few or a whole dozen. Do not freeze.

1. **Large eggs**
   Cold water, to cover

You will need: a medium saucepan and a timer or clock.

1. Place the eggs in the saucepan. Cover with the water. Heat on medium-high until the water boils. The lid may be on or off. It will boil faster with it on but it is easier to see when it starts to boil with it off. When the water is boiling rapidly, set the timer for 10 minutes. Turn the heat down if needed but keep the water boiling. Drain. Cover the eggs with cold water. Drain when the water gets warm which will be only a few moments. Re-cover with cold water. Repeat until the eggs are room temperature. Crack the large end of the egg and peel, dipping in water now and then. Or leave the shells on until you are ready to eat the eggs. Store, covered, in the refrigerator. Makes from 1 to a potful.

Variation: To make colored eggs, let hard-boiled eggs soak for at least half an hour in bowls of hot water with different colors in each. Use food coloring. Remove the eggs and let them dry on paper towels. When they are completely dry, put a drop of cooking oil in the palms of your hands and rub over each egg to give it a shine and set the color.

Macaroni Salad

This one has a crunch to it with added cabbage. Strips of pimiento can be added for color. Do not freeze.

1.
Water	3 qts.	3 L
Cooking oil	1 tbsp.	15 mL
Salt	2 tsp.	10 mL
Elbow macaroni	2 cups	500 mL

2.
Coarsely grated cabbage	2 cups	500 mL
Chopped celery	½ cup	125 mL
Onion flakes	2 tbsp.	30 mL
Parsley flakes	1 tsp.	5 mL

3.
Salad dressing (or mayonnaise)	1 cup	250 mL
Salt	1 tsp.	5 mL
Pepper	⅛ tsp.	0.5 mL
Granulated sugar	1 tsp.	5 mL
Milk	¼ cup	50 mL

You will need: a large saucepan or Dutch oven, measuring spoons, measuring cups, a mixing spoon, a colander, a large bowl, a small bowl and a small mixing spoon.

1. Bring the water to a boil in the saucepan on medium-high heat. Add the cooking oil and salt. Add the macaroni. Stir occasionally as it cooks. Heat may need to be turned down but keep it boiling for 5 to 10 minutes until tender but firm. Drain into the colander in the sink. Run cold water over the macaroni to stop the cooking process and to cool. Drain well. Turn into the large bowl.

2. Add the cabbage, celery, onion flakes and parsley flakes. Stir.

3. Stir the salad dressing, salt, pepper and sugar together in the small bowl . Pour over the macaroni mixture. Stir. Let stand in the refrigerator about ½ to 1 hour or longer to cool completely and blend flavors. Makes about 7 cups (1.7 L).

Pictured on page 83.

1. Potato Salad
2. Macaroni Salad page 82

Potato Salad

Grated carrot adds crunchiness to this salad. Do not freeze.

1. **Medium potatoes, peeled and**   **5**   **5**
      quartered
   Water, to cover

2. **Hard-boiled eggs, (see page 81),**   **4**   **4**
      peeled and chopped

Chopped celery	**½ cup**	**125 mL**
Peeled and grated carrot	**¼ cup**	**50 mL**
Onion flakes	**2 tbsp.**	**30 mL**

3.
Salad dressing (or mayonnaise)	**1 cup**	**250 mL**
Milk	**¼ cup**	**50 mL**
Granulated sugar	**1 tsp.**	**5 mL**
Salt	**1 tsp.**	**5 mL**
Pepper	**¼ tsp.**	**1 mL**

You will need: a medium saucepan, a sharp knife, a large bowl, measuring spoons, measuring cups, a mixing spoon, a small bowl and a small spoon.

1. Cook the potatoes in the water in the saucepan until tender. Drain. Cool until you can handle them, then cut them into cubes about the size of sugar cubes. Put the potato into the large bowl.

2. Add the next 4 ingredients to the potatoes. Stir to mix.

3. Put the salad dressing, milk, sugar, salt and pepper into the small bowl. Stir well. Pour over the potato mixture. Stir to coat. Let stand in the refrigerator for at least 1 hour to allow the flavors to mix. Serves 6 to 8.

Pictured above.

Sandwiches

Variety is important unless you only like one kind of sandwich. However, if you finally get bored with it, here are several to take its place. Do not freeze.

BAKED BEAN SANDWICH: Spread beans, drained, on 1 slice of buttered bread. Add some chopped cooked sausage, ground meat or wieners if available. You can try mashing the beans before spreading if you like. Cover with the second slice of buttered bread.

BEEF SANDWICH: Spread 1 slice of buttered bread with mustard, ketchup or salad dressing (or mayonnaise). Top with slices of cold roast beef. Add some lettuce or alfalfa sprouts if desired. Be sure to put lettuce on the beef side not touching the salad dressing. It stays crisper. Cover with the second slice of buttered bread. See ❻ page 85.

CHEESE AND LETTUCE SANDWICH: Spread 1 slice of buttered bread with salad dressing (or mayonnaise) or sandwich spread. Lay a cheese slice over top. Place some lettuce on the cheese. Do not put the lettuce on the salad dressing or it will wilt. Cover with the second slice of buttered bread. See ❸ page 85.

CHEESE AND TOMATO SANDWICH: On 1 buttered slice of bread, spread sandwich spread or salad dressing (or mayonnaise). Lay a cheese slice over top then cover the cheese with tomato slices. Sprinkle with salt and pepper if desired. Cover with the second slice of buttered bread. See ❺ page 85.

CHEESE SANDWICH: Cut a slice of Swiss or Cheddar cheese to fit 1 slice of buttered bread. Sandwich spread or salad dressing (or mayonnaise) is a good additional spread. Cover with the second buttered slice of buttered bread. Or use a processed cheese spread instead of the cheese slice. See ❷ page 85.

CHICKEN SANDWICH OR ROLL: Butter 2 slices of bread or the inside surfaces of a roll. If you have some leftover cooked chicken in the refrigerator, slice enough to cover one bread slice. A bit of cranberry sauce or some leftover stuffing can be added. Top with the second slice of bread.

HAM AND CHEESE SANDWICH: On 1 slice of buttered bread spread mustard, salad dressing (or mayonnaise) or sandwich spread. Add a slice of ham, then a slice of cheese. Cover with the second slice of buttered bread. See ❹ page 85.

(continued on next page)

HAM AND LETTUCE SANDWICH: Spread 1 slice of buttered bread with mustard or salad dressing (or mayonnaise). Put a slice of ham over top. Add some lettuce. Cover with the second slice of buttered bread.

HAM & TOMATO SANDWICH: On 1 slice of buttered bread, spread mustard, salad dressing (or mayonnaise) or sandwich spread. Add a slice of ham, then a slice of tomato. Cover with the second slice of buttered bread.

HAMBURGER: Insert a cooked meat patty into a buttered hamburger bun. Add ketchup, onions, pickles, relish, cheese, mustard, tomatoes or whatever else you like.

HOT DOG: Insert a hot wiener into a buttered hot dog bun. Add ketchup, relish and mustard. Onions are good, too. A delicious hot dog has a narrow slice of cheese and a slice of cooked bacon along side of the wiener.

PBBS: Do try a Peanut Butter Banana Sandwich. Spread 1 slice of buttered bread with peanut butter. Put a layer of banana slices over top. Cover with the second slice of buttered bread. Delicious. See ❶ below.

PEANUT BUTTER SANDWICH: Spread 1 slice of buttered bread with peanut butter. Cover with the second slice of buttered bread. If you prefer, spread the second slice of buttered bread with honey, jam or jelly before placing over the peanut butter.

SUBMARINE: Split and butter a submarine bun. Layer it with your favorite cheese slice, cold meat slices, sliced tomato, lettuce, salad dressing (or mayonnaise) and mustard.

Egg Filling

Add a piece of lettuce for color. Do not freeze.

1. **Large hard-boiled eggs, (see**   4   4
    page 81), peeled and finely
    chopped or mashed

Sweet pickle relish	2 tsp.	10 mL
Salt	¼ tsp.	1 mL
Onion powder	¼ tsp.	1 mL
Salad dressing (or mayonnaise)	2 tbsp.	30 mL

You will need: measuring spoons, a small bowl and a mixing spoon.

1. Place all of the ingredients in the bowl. Stir them together well. Makes about 1 cup (250 mL), enough for 4 to 5 sandwiches.

Tuna Filling

So quick to make. Add a few alfalfa sprouts.

1. **Canned tuna in water, drained**	6.5 oz.	184 g
Diced celery	¼ cup	50 mL
Diced apple, with peel	¼ cup	50 mL
Onion powder	¼ tsp.	1 mL
Salad dressing (or mayonnaise)	1½ tbsp.	25 mL

You will need: measuring spoons, measuring cups, a small bowl and a mixing spoon.

1. Combine all of the ingredients in the bowl. Mix well. Makes a generous 1 cup (250 mL), enough for 4 to 5 sandwiches.

Chicken Filling

Great use for leftover chicken.

1.			
Chopped cooked chicken (or 6.5 oz., 184 g, canned flaked chicken)		1 cup	250 mL
Chopped celery		¼ cup	50 mL
Peeled and grated carrot		¼ cup	50 mL
Salad dressing (or mayonnaise)		2 tbsp.	30 mL

You will need: measuring spoons, measuring cups, a small bowl and a mixing spoon.

1. Combine all of the ingredients in the small bowl. Stir together well. Makes a generous 1 cup (250 mL), enough for 4 to 5 sandwiches.

Salmon Filling

Excellent in croissants, too!

1.		
Canned salmon, drained, skin and round bones removed	7¼ oz.	220 g
Sweet pickle relish	2 tsp.	10 mL
Parsley flakes	½ tsp.	2 mL
Onion powder	¼ tsp.	1 mL
Salt	⅛ tsp.	0.5 mL
Salad dressing (or mayonnaise)	3 tbsp.	45 mL

You will need: measuring spoons, a small bowl and a mixing spoon.

1. Combine all of the ingredients in the small bowl. Stir together well. Makes about 1 cup (250 mL), enough for 4 to 5 sandwiches.

Meaty Buns

This makes enough to serve your friends, too. Pictured on page 89.

1.			
Canned Prem, Spam, Kam, Klik, or Spork, mashed	12 oz.	341 g
Grated medium Cheddar cheese	2 cups	500 mL
Medium green pepper, seeded and finely chopped	1	1
Condensed tomato soup	10 oz.	284 mL
Worcestershire sauce	2 tsp.	10 mL
Sweet pickle relish	2 tbsp.	30 mL
Onion salt	½ tsp.	2 mL

You will need: measuring spoons, measuring cups, a medium bowl, a mixing spoon and a table knife.

1. Combine all of the ingredients in the bowl. Mix well. Spread over split hamburger buns and broil. You can also split a French loaf lengthwise then spread each half with this filling. Broil to heat and to melt the cheese. You could also fill hamburger buns, wrap each in foil and heat for about 15 minutes in a 350°F (175°C) oven until hot. Makes 4 cups (1 L) of filling.

Grilled Cheese Sandwich

This is easy to make for the whole family. Good to eat with or without a bowl of soup. Pictured on page 89.

1.			
Bread slices, white or brown	2	2
Butter or hard margarine, softened (at room temperature)	1 tbsp.	15 mL
Yellow cheese slice	1	1

You will need: an electric frying pan or a regular frying pan, a dinner knife, a pancake lifter, a small plate and a sharp knife.

1. Heat the electric frying pan to 340° (170°C) or heat a regular frying pan to medium-hot. Lay the bread slices on the counter. Butter both slices on one side. Place 1 slice, buttered side down, in the frying pan. Put the cheese slice on top. Cover with the second bread slice with buttered side up. When the bottom side is browned, flip the sandwich over to brown the other side. Use the lifter to remove the sandwich to the plate. Cut in half. Enjoy with your favorite pickles. Makes 1 sandwich.

Scrambled Egg Sandwich

A quick sandwich for a lunch or snack. Do not freeze.

1. **Bread slices, buttered on one side**	**2**	**2**
2. **SCRAMBLED EGG**		
Butter or hard margarine	**½ tsp.**	**2 mL**
Large egg (see Note)	**1**	**1**
Water	**1 tbsp.**	**15 mL**
3. **Salt, sprinkle (optional)**		
Pepper, sprinkle (optional)		
Ketchup	**2 tsp.**	**10 mL**

You will need: measuring spoons, a small frying pan, a table fork, a table knife, a pancake lifter and a small plate.

1. Lay bread slices, buttered side up, on the counter.

2. Scrambled Egg: Put the butter or margarine into the frying pan on medium heat. Add the egg and water. Beat with the fork. Stir continually as it cooks.

3. When cooked, spread over 1 slice of the bread. Sprinkle with the salt and pepper. Spread the ketchup on the second slice of bread or, if it is in a squeeze bottle, squeeze directly onto the scrambled egg. Place the second slice over top of the first. Cut in half. Transfer to the plate. Makes 1 sandwich.

Scrambled Eggs: For 2 to 3 servings, use 1 tbsp. (15 mL) butter or hard margarine, 4 eggs, 3 tbsp. (45 mL) water (or milk), ¼ tsp. (1 mL) of salt and a sprinkle of pepper.

Pictured below.

1. Meaty Buns page 88
2. Grilled Cheese Sandwich page 88
3. Scrambled Egg Sandwich

Platter Courtesy Of:
Le Gnome

Trail Mix

A simple mix to have for munching. Good for a bagged lunch, too.

1.	**Butter or hard margarine**	**1 tbsp.**	**15 mL**
	Peanuts	**1 cup**	**250 mL**
	Sunflower seeds	**¼ cup**	**50 mL**
2.	**Raisins**	**1¼ cups**	**300 mL**
	Dried apricots, cut in 4 to 6 pieces each	**⅔ cup**	**150 mL**
	Salt, sprinkle		

You will need: measuring spoons, a frying pan, measuring cups, a mixing spoon, a large bowl and a container with a lid.

1. Melt butter or margarine in the frying pan on medium heat. Add peanuts and sunflower seeds. Stir often as they brown. When they look browned, pour them into the bowl. Cool.

2. Add the raisins and apricots to the bowl. Stir. Sprinkle with salt. Stir. Taste. Add a bit more salt if needed. Store in the container. Makes about 3 cups (750 mL).

Beef Jerky

You will need a pocket full of this if you're going on a hike. Great at camp fires, too!

1.	**Sirloin or top round steak, 1 inch (2.5 cm) thick**	1 lb.	454 g
2.	**Water**	½ cup	125 mL
	Envelope of dry onion soup mix	1 x 1½ oz.	1 x 42 g
	Liquid smoke	1 tsp.	5 mL
	Garlic powder	¼ tsp.	1 mL
	Salt	¼ tsp.	1 mL
	Pepper	⅛ tsp.	0.5 mL

You will need: a sharp knife, a cutting board, a plastic bag, measuring spoons, measuring cups, a small bowl, a mixing spoon, paper towels, wire racks, a cookie sheet, oven mitts and a pair of tongs.

1. Cut all the visible fat from the meat. Cut the meat into long strips about ⅛ inch (3 mm) thick. This is easier to do if you partially freeze the meat first. Put the strips into the plastic bag.

2. Measure the remaining 6 ingredients into the small bowl. Stir together well. Pour into the bag over the meat. Remove as much air as you can from the bag. Seal with a twist tie. Squeeze to get all beef wet with marinade. Place the bag in the refrigerator, turning occasionally, for at least 6 hours or overnight. Turn the oven on to 150°F (65°C). Remove the beef from the marinade. Blot with some paper towels. Place the wire rack in the cookie sheet. Arrange the meat strips on the rack. Dry on the center rack in the oven for 4 hours. Use the oven mitts to remove the pan from the oven. Turn the beef strips over with the tongs. Continue to dry the strips in the oven for 3 or 4 more hours until the strips begin to get brittle. Use the oven mitts to remove the cookie sheet to the second wire rack. Cool completely. This keeps well. Freeze the jerky for long-term storage or keep the jerky refrigerated.

Apple Leather

Like fruit roll-ups. All you need is patience.

1.
Canned applesauce	**14 oz.**	**398 mL**
Granulated sugar, or honey	**1 tbsp.**	**15 mL**
Ground cinnamon	**¹⁄₈ tsp.**	**0.5 mL**

You will need: measuring spoons, a small bowl, a mixing spoon, a 10 x 15 inch (25 x 38 cm) jelly roll pan, plastic wrap, a rubber spatula, oven mitts and a wire rack.

1. Turn the oven on to 150°F (65°C). Mix the applesauce, sugar or honey and cinnamon together in the bowl. Line the jelly roll pan with plastic wrap. If you dampen your hand under the tap and then dampen the pan with your hand, the plastic wrap will stick quite well. Spread the applesauce mixture evenly in the pan not quite to the edges using the rubber spatula. This is so thin it is hard to spread without holes appearing. Place the pan on the center rack in the oven. It will take about 7 hours to dry. Use the oven mitts to turn the pan around in the oven after 3 or 4 hours. You will know it is done when it feels leathery and it will lift away from the plastic. Use the oven mitts to remove the pan to the wire rack. Cool for about 5 minutes. Roll up. Cover the roll of leather with plastic wrap.

PEACH LEATHER: Drain two 14 oz. (398 mL) cans of sliced peaches. Purée the peaches in a blender until smooth. Use instead of the applesauce.

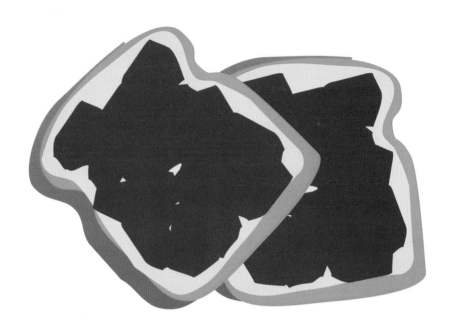

Cinnamon Toast Spread

A real treat. This was a staple in our house for after school snacks and is now my grandchildrens' favorite.

1.	**Butter or hard margarine**	$^1/_3$ **cup**	**75 mL**
	Granulated sugar	$^2/_3$ **cup**	**150 mL**
	Ground cinnamon	**1 tbsp.**	**15 mL**

You will need: measuring spoons, measuring cups, a small saucepan, a mixing spoon, a hot pad and a small container with a lid.

1. Put all 3 ingredients into the saucepan on medium heat. Stir until the butter or margarine melts. Remove the saucepan to the hot pad. Let the mixture cool in the saucepan. The butter or margarine will rise to the top. When it is cool, stir well and store it in the container. Makes about $^3/_4$ cup (175 mL). Spread about 1 tbsp. (15 mL) on hot slice of toast.

Variation: Combine only the sugar and cinnamon and sprinkle as much as you like on warm, buttered toast. Store in the container.

Nachos

For a mild nacho, make this without the chilies or keep them in for a robust flavor. Use one or both cheeses. Do not freeze.

1.	Tortilla chips	2 oz.	60 g
2.	Grated mild or medium Cheddar cheese	⅓ cup	75 mL
	Grated Monterey Jack cheese	⅓ cup	75 mL
	Green onion, thinly sliced	1	1
	Green or black olives, sliced	4	4
	Chopped green chilies or Jalapeño peppers (canned or fresh), optional		
3.	Salsa	¼ cup	50 mL
	Sour cream	¼ cup	50 mL

You will need: a cookie sheet, measuring cups, oven mitts and a wire rack.

1. Turn the oven on to 350°F (175°C). Crowd the tortilla chips on the cookie sheet.

2. Sprinkle with both the cheeses, the green onion and sliced olives. If you are using the green chilies or jalapeño peppers, scatter them over the nachos. Bake on the center rack in the oven for about 3 minutes to melt the cheese. Use the oven mitts to remove the cookie sheet to the wire rack.

3. Serve with the salsa and/or sour cream to use as a dip. Serves 1 hungry snacker.

Pictured above.

Nacho Two Step

This is worth hurrying home from school to make. Recipe may be halved if desired. Do not freeze.

1.	**Tortilla chips**	**8 oz.**	**224 g**
2.	**Medium tomatoes**	**2**	**2**
	Canned chopped green chilies, drained	**4 oz.**	**114 mL**
	Sliced green onions	**¼ cup**	**50 mL**
	Chili powder	**½ tsp.**	**2 mL**
	Grated mild or medium Cheddar cheese	**¼ cup**	**50 mL**
3.	**Grated Monterey Jack cheese**	**2 cups**	**500 mL**

You will need: a cookie sheet, a sharp knife, a small spoon, a medium bowl, measuring spoons, measuring cups, a mixing spoon, oven mitts and a wire rack.

1. Turn the oven on to 350°F (175°C). Pour the tortilla chips onto the cookie sheet. Crowd them together so you don't see much of the cookie sheet under them.

2. Cut the tomatoes in half. Squeeze each half lightly to remove the seeds. Use the small spoon to help. Throw away the seeds. Dice the two halves into the bowl. Add the green chilies, green onions, chili powder and Cheddar cheese. Stir. Spoon over the chips.

3. Sprinkle the remaining cheese over top. Bake on the center rack in the oven for about 10 minutes until hot and the cheese is melted. Use the oven mitts to remove the cookie sheet to the wire rack. Serves 2 hungry appetites.

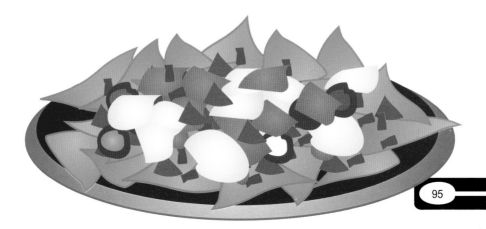

Jelly Jiggles

Great for parties! Do not freeze.

1. **Envelopes of unflavored gelatin**	**2 × ¼ oz.**	**2 × 7 g**
Orange-flavored gelatin (jelly powder)	**2 × 3 oz.**	**2 × 85 g**
2. **Boiling water**	**2½ cups**	**625 mL**

You will need: a medium bowl, a mixing spoon, a tea kettle, measuring cups and a 9 x 13 inch (22 x 33 cm) pan.

1. Pour both the unflavored and flavored gelatins into the bowl. Stir well.

2. Add the boiling water to the bowl. Stir until the gelatins are dissolved. Pour into the pan. Place the lightly greased pan, uncovered, in the refrigerator for at least 3 hours until set. Cut into whatever shapes you desire.

Pictured below.

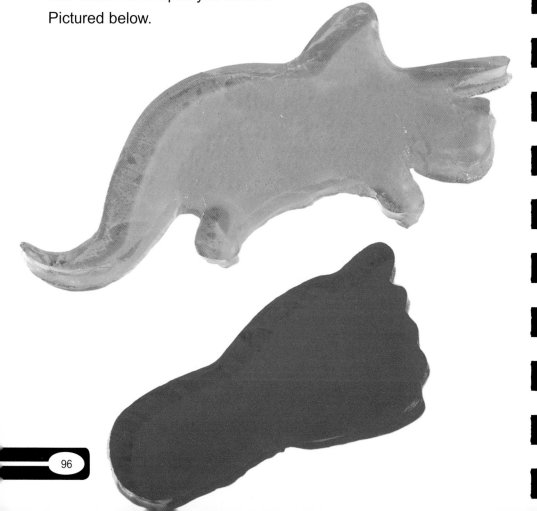

Creamy Jelly Jiggles

These jiggles settle into layers for a different look. Do not freeze.

1.	**Envelopes of unflavored gelatin**	**2 × ¼ oz.**	**2 × 7 g**
	Lime-flavored gelatin (jelly powder)	**2 × 3 oz.**	**2 × 85 g**
2.	**Boiling water**	**1²/₃ cups**	**400 mL**
3.	**Half and half (light cream)**	**²/₃ cup**	**150 mL**

You will need: a medium bowl, a mixing spoon, a tea kettle, measuring cups and a 9 × 13 inch (22 × 33 cm) pan.

1. Pour both the unflavored and the flavored gelatins into the bowl. Stir well.

2. Add the boiling water to gelatin in the bowl. Stir until the gelatins dissolve.

3. Add the half and half. Stir. Pour into the lightly greased pan. Chill in the refrigerator for at least 3 hours. Cut into squares or use cookie cutters to cut into your favorite shapes.

Pictured below.

Jiffy Pizza

A good quick pizza snack.

1.	**Bacon slices**	2	2
2.	**Ketchup**	2 tbsp.	30 mL
	Dried oregano	¼ tsp.	1 mL
	Onion powder	¼ tsp.	1 mL
3.	**Hamburger bun, split and buttered**	1	1
4.	**Yellow cheese slice**	2	2
	Mozzarella cheese slice	2	2

You will need: a frying pan, a sharp knife, a sheet of paper towel, measuring spoons, a small cup, a small mixing spoon, a broiler pan, a table knife, oven mitts and a wire rack.

1. Fry the bacon in the frying pan on medium-low heat. Cut the bacon slices in half crosswise or cut in small pieces. Drain on the paper towel.

2. Stir the ketchup, oregano and onion powder in the small cup.

3. Place the 2 bun halves on the broiler pan. Spread the ketchup mixture over the 2 bun halves.

4. Lay the yellow cheese slice then the white cheese slice (or vice versa) over each bun half. Now lay the short pieces of bacon over each. Put the pan on the top rack in the oven. Broil for 1 to 2 minutes to melt the cheese. Watch carefully so that it doesn't burn. Use the oven mitts to remove the pan to the wire rack. Serves 1.

Pictured on the front cover and below.

Vegetable Beef Soup

Definitely a meal in itself. A very filling soup.

1.	**Cooking oil**	**2 tsp.**	**10 mL**
	Lean ground beef	**½ lb.**	**225 g**
2.	**Canned tomatoes, broken up, with juice**	**14 oz.**	**398 mL**
	Frozen mixed vegetables	**10 oz.**	**284 g**
	Peeled and diced onion	**1 cup**	**250 mL**
	Water	**4 cups**	**1 L**
	Beef bouillon powder	**1 tbsp.**	**15 mL**
	Salt	**1 tsp.**	**5 mL**
	Pepper	**¼ tsp.**	**1 mL**
	Ground thyme	**¼ tsp.**	**1 mL**

You will need: measuring spoons, a large saucepan, a mixing spoon and measuring cups.

1. Place the cooking oil and ground beef in the saucepan over medium heat. Scramble-fry the meat until browned and crumbly.

2. Add the remaining ingredients. Stir. Bring the soup to a boil. Cover. Boil slowly, turning down the heat as needed. Simmer about 20 minutes, until the vegetables are tender. Serve with crackers, crusty rolls or sandwiches. Makes about 8½ cups (2 L).

Soup Bowl And Plate Courtesy Of:
The Bay China Dept.

Chicken Barley Soup

Easy to assemble and cook. Excellent soup.

1.
Water	**5 cups**	**1.25 L**
Chicken bouillon powder	**5 tsp.**	**25 mL**
Peeled and diced carrot	**½ cup**	**125 mL**
Peeled and diced potato	**½ cup**	**125 mL**
Peeled and diced onion	**½ cup**	**125 mL**
Barley	**½ cup**	**125 mL**
Canned tomatoes, broken up, with juice	**14 oz.**	**398 mL**

2.
Canned chicken or turkey flakes, mashed or flaked	**6.5 oz.**	**184 g**

You will need: measuring spoons, measuring cups, a large saucepan and a mixing spoon.

1. Put the first 7 ingredients into the saucepan. Stir. Heat on medium-high, stirring often as it comes to a boil. Cover. Turn down the heat so it boils slowly for about 1 hour. Stir occasionally as it simmers.

2. Add the chicken or turkey. Simmer a few more minutes. Serve with crackers. Makes 6½ cups (1.6 L).

Pictured above.

Brownies

This is an all-time favorite for lunches, snacks, dessert or just for fun.

1.	Butter or hard margarine	½ cup	125 mL
	Semisweet chocolate chips	1 cup	250 mL
2.	Large eggs	2	2
	Brown sugar, packed	½ cup	125 mL
	Vanilla flavoring	1 tsp.	5 mL
3.	All-purpose flour	1 cup	250 mL
	Chopped walnuts	½ cup	125 mL

You will need: an 8 x 8 inch (20 x 20 cm) pan, measuring cups, a small saucepan, 2 mixing spoons, a hot pad, a medium bowl, measuring spoons, a rubber spatula, oven mitts and a wire rack.

1. Turn the oven on to 350°F (175°C). Grease the pan. Combine the butter or margarine and the chocolate chips in the saucepan. Place on low heat. Stir often until they are melted. Do not overheat. Remove the saucepan to the hot pad.

2. Beat the eggs with the other spoon in the mixing bowl until frothy. Add the sugar and vanilla flavoring. Beat to mix. Add the chocolate mixture. Stir.

3. Add the flour and walnuts. Stir just until moistened. Turn the batter into the pan. Spread evenly with the rubber spatula. Bake on the center rack in the oven for about 25 minutes. A wooden toothpick inserted in the center should come out moist but not wet with batter. Use the oven mitts to remove the pan to the wire rack. Cool Brownies completely before icing. Cuts into 25 squares.

Crispy Roll

Crisp cereal rolled together with a yummy chocolate filling. A scene stealer. Pictured on the front cover and below.

1.	Light corn syrup	1 cup	250 mL
	Granulated sugar	1 cup	250 mL
	Smooth peanut butter	1 cup	250 mL
	Butter or hard margarine	3 tbsp.	45 mL
2.	Crisp rice cereal	6 cups	1.5 L
3.	FILLING		
	Butter or hard margarine, softened (at room temperature)	½ cup	125 mL
	Icing (confectioner's) sugar	2 cups	500 mL
	Cocoa	1 cup	250 mL
	Water	¼ cup	50 mL
	Vanilla flavoring	1 tsp.	5 mL

You will need: measuring spoons, measuring cups, a large saucepan, 2 mixing spoons, a hot pad, waxed paper, a medium bowl, an electric mixer, a rubber spatula, a table knife and plastic wrap.

1. Put the syrup, sugar, peanut butter and butter or margarine into the saucepan. Bring to a boil over medium-high heat, stirring constantly. Remove the saucepan to the hot pad.

2. Mix in the rice cereal until coated. Place the waxed paper on the counter that has been dampened with water so paper will stay in place. Press the cereal mixture into a rectangle about 10 x 15 inch (25 x 38 cm) on the waxed paper. Let stand for 15 to 20 minutes before putting on the filling. Edges should be room temperature. Center should still be warm.

3. Filling: Put all 5 ingredients into the bowl and beat on medium speed until smooth, adding a bit more water if it is too thick to spread. Spread over the rice cereal mixture using the rubber spatula and the table knife. Roll as for a jelly roll starting at the narrow end using the waxed paper to help. Wrap in plastic wrap and chill. Slice thinly to serve. Cuts into 24 slices.

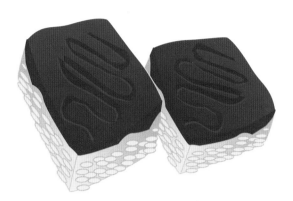

Crispy Squares

Crunchy and very good.

1.	**Brown sugar, packed** **Light or dark corn syrup**	1 cup 1 cup	250 mL 250 mL
2.	**Smooth peanut butter**	1 cup	250 mL
3.	**Crisp rice cereal**	6 cups	1.5 L
4.	**ICING** **Semisweet chocolate chips** **Butterscotch chips** **Butter or hard margarine**	 1 cup 1 cup 2 tbsp.	 250 mL 250 mL 30 mL

You will need: measuring cups, 2 medium saucepans, 2 mixing spoons, a hot pad, a rubber spatula, a 9 × 13 inch (22 × 33 cm) pan, measuring spoons and a large bowl.

1. Measure the brown sugar and syrup into the first saucepan over medium heat. Stir until it starts to boil. Remove the saucepan to the hot pad.

2. Stir in the peanut butter until the mixture is smooth.

3. Put the rice cereal into the bowl. Pour the peanut butter mixture over the top, using the spatula to get every last bit of mixture. Stir well to coat all of the cereal. Grease the pan. Pack the mixture into the pan.

4. Icing: Place both kinds of chips and butter or margarine in the other saucepan over low heat. Stir often. Be sure to keep the heat low. When the chips have melted, spread over the squares. Let set. Cuts into 54 squares or 27 bars.

Crisp Crunchies

You will think you are eating a candy bar.

1.			
Smooth peanut butter	1 cup	250 mL
Icing (confectioner's) sugar	1¾ cups	425 mL
Ground peanuts	½ cup	125 mL
Butter or hard margarine, softened (at room temperature)	⅓ cup	75 mL

2.			
Crisp rice cereal, crushed (measure before crushing)	2 cups	500 mL

3.	COATING		
Semisweet chocolate chips	⅔ cup	150 mL
Butter or hard margarine	2 tbsp.	30 mL

You will need: measuring cups, a medium bowl, a plastic bag, a rolling pin, measuring spoons, a rubber spatula, a 9 x 9 inch (22 x 22 cm) pan, 2 mixing spoons, a water glass, a heavy small saucepan and a rubber spatula.

1. Combine the peanut butter, icing sugar, peanuts and butter or margarine in the bowl. Set aside.

2. Put the rice cereal into the plastic bag. Roll with the rolling pin to crush well. Add to the bowl. Mix well. You may have to use your hands. Press into the greased pan. Use the water glass to roll it flat. Put the pan into the refrigerator. Chill until firm.

3. Coating: Melt the chocolate chips and the butter or margarine in the saucepan on low heat. Stir often until it is smooth. Remove the pan from the refrigerator. Pour the chocolate coating over top of the squares in the pan using the rubber spatula to remove all of the chocolate. Let stand to set the chocolate. Cuts into 36 squares or 18 bars.

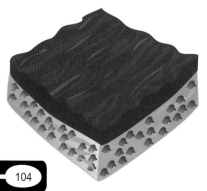

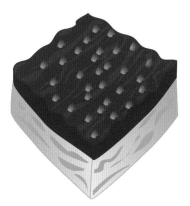

Crunchy Fudge

Soft and chewy. Tastes like a candy bar.

1.	**Butter or hard margarine**	**1 cup**	**250 mL**
	Brown sugar, packed	**1 cup**	**250 mL**
	Vanilla flavoring	**½ tsp.**	**2 mL**
2.	**Quick rolled oats**	**3 cups**	**750 mL**
	Light or dark corn syrup	**½ cup**	**125 mL**
	All-purpose flour	**1 cup**	**250 mL**
3.	**SECOND LAYER**		
	Semisweet chocolate chips	**1 cup**	**250 mL**
	Smooth peanut butter	**¾ cup**	**175 mL**
	Ground or very finely chopped peanuts	**⅓ cup**	**75 mL**

You will need: measuring spoons, measuring cups, a large saucepan, 2 mixing spoons, a hot pad, a 9 x 13 inch (22 x 33 cm) pan, a rubber spatula, oven mitts, a wire rack and a medium saucepan.

1. Turn the oven on to 350°F (175°C). Place the butter or margarine, brown sugar and vanilla flavoring in the large saucepan. Stir over medium heat until the butter is melted and the sugar is mixed in well. Remove the saucepan to the hot pad.

2. Add the rolled oats, syrup and flour. Stir together well. Grease the pan. Scrape the mixture into the pan. Spread it to make it level and smooth. Bake on the center rack in the oven for 15 minutes. Use the oven mitts to remove the pan to the wire rack. Cool slightly before adding the second layer.

3. Second Layer: Combine the chocolate chips, peanut butter and peanuts in the medium saucepan. Place on low heat. Stir often until the chips are melted. Spread over the bottom layer. Let stand until set. Cuts into 54 squares or 27 bars.

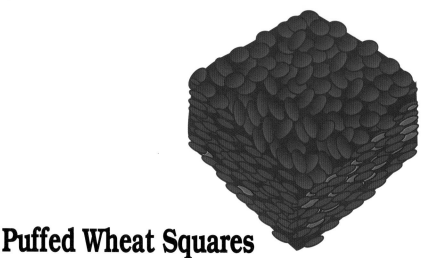

Puffed Wheat Squares

Try your best to share this. It will be hard to do.

1.	Butter or hard margarine	⅓ cup	75 mL
	Light or dark corn syrup	½ cup	125 mL
	Brown sugar, packed	⅔ cup	150 mL
	Cocoa	2 tbsp.	30 mL
	Vanilla flavoring	1 tsp.	5 mL
2.	Puffed wheat	8 cups	2 L

You will need: measuring spoons, measuring cups, a medium saucepan, a mixing spoon, a hot pad, a very large bowl, a rubber spatula and a 9 × 9 inch (22 × 22 cm) pan.

1. Combine the butter or margarine, syrup, brown sugar, cocoa and vanilla flavoring in the saucepan. Stir continually on medium heat until it starts to boil with bubbles all over the surface. Remove the saucepan to the hot pad.

2. Measure the puffed wheat into the bowl. Pour the hot chocolate mixture over the top. Use the rubber spatula to scrape the saucepan. Stir well until all of the puffed wheat is coated. Grease the pan. Turn the coated puffed wheat into the pan. Press down using the dampened spatula. Chill for about 2 hours so it will cut cleanly. Cuts into 16 or 25 squares.

Pictured on page 107.

Crispy Rice Squares

An old-time favorite.

1.	**Butter or hard margarine**	**¼ cup**	**50 mL**
	Large marshmallows (about 35)	**9 oz.**	**250 g**
2.	**Crisp rice cereal**	**6 cups**	**1.5 L**

You will need: measuring cups, a large saucepan or a Dutch oven, a mixing spoon, a hot pad, a 9 x 9 inch (22 x 22 cm) pan and a rubber spatula.

1. Put the butter or margarine and the marshmallows into the saucepan. Heat on medium, stirring often until it is melted. Remove the saucepan to the hot pad.

2. Add the rice cereal. Stir well until all of the cereal is coated. Grease the pan. Scrape out all of the cereal into the pan. Press down firmly using the dampened rubber spatula. Chill about 2 hours before cutting. Cuts into 16 or 25 squares.

Pictured below.

1. Puffed Wheat Squares page 106
2. Crispy Rice Squares

Bowls Courtesy Of:
Selfridge Pottery Studio

Baked Potatoes

The fastest preparation with the least "hands on".

1. **Medium baking potatoes**   **4-6**   **4-6**

You will need: a sharp knife.

1. Turn the oven on to 400°F (205°C). Wash and dry the potatoes. Jab each potato in 2 or 3 places on each side with the tip of the knife. This prevents them from bursting in the oven. If you want a softer skin when finished, rub the skins with butter or margarine or wrap each potato in foil. Place the potatoes on the center rack in the oven. Bake for about 45 to 60 minutes. Stick the potatoes with the knife to see if they are soft. You can also test by holding one potato in a pot holder or a paper napkin and squeezing to see if it is soft. Serves 4 to 6 or as many as you bake potatoes for.

Mashed Potatoes

Always a welcome comfort food.

1. **Water**
       Medium potatoes   6   6

2. **Milk, hot is best**   ½ cup   125 mL
       Salt   ½ tsp.   2 mL
       Pepper   ⅛ tsp.   0.5 mL
       Onion salt   ½ tsp.   2 mL
       Butter or hard margarine   2 tbsp.   30 mL

You will need: a large saucepan, a vegetable peeler, a sharp knife, a potato masher, measuring spoons and measuring cups.

1. Pour enough water into the saucepan to be 1 inch (2.5 cm) deep. Peel the potatoes and then cut each potato into 4 pieces. Place the potatoes into the water in the saucepan. Cover. Bring to a boil over medium heat. When the water starts to boil, turn the heat to low. Simmer slowly for 20 to 30 minutes. To test the potatoes, stick the knife into several pieces. The potatoes should feel soft and tender. Drain well.

2. Break up the potatoes with the potato masher. Add all of the remaining ingredients and mash well. Serves 4 to 6.

Casserole Dish Courtesy Of:
Selfridge Pottery Studio

Flavorful Rice

Extra flavorful and extra attractive. Peas add spots of color throughout.

1.			
	Long grain rice	1 cup	250 mL
	Chopped onion	½ cup	125 mL
	Chicken bouillon powder	1 tsp.	5 mL
	Water	2 cups	500 mL
	Salt	½ tsp.	2 mL
2.	Water	½ cup	125 mL
	Frozen peas	1 cup	250 mL

You will need: measuring spoons, measuring cups, a medium saucepan, a small saucepan and a mixing spoon.

1. Measure the first 5 ingredients into the medium saucepan. Put on the lid. Heat on medium high until it starts to boil. Turn the heat down so that it will simmer slowly for 15 minutes until the rice is tender and the water is absorbed. Do not lift the lid while the rice is cooking.

2. Put the remaining water and peas into the small saucepan. Cover and heat on medium-high until it starts to boil. Turn down the heat. Simmer gently for 3 minutes. Drain. Stir the peas into the rice. Serves 4.

Pictured above.

Saucy Corn

Decked out in a white sauce with little green and red bits show-ing. Good and colorful. Pictured on page 111.

1.	Butter or hard margarine	2 tbsp.	30 mL
	All-purpose flour	2 tbsp.	30 mL
	Salt	½ tsp.	2 mL
	Pepper	⅛ tsp.	0.5 mL
	Milk	1 cup	250 mL
2.	Kernel corn, drained	12 oz.	341 mL
	Seeded and finely chopped green pepper	1 tbsp.	15 mL
	Finely chopped pimiento (or red pepper)	1 tbsp.	15 mL

You will need: measuring spoons, a medium saucepan, mea-suring cups and a mixing spoon.

1. Melt the butter or margarine in the saucepan. Mix in the flour, salt and pepper. Add the milk. Stir until it boils and thickens.

2. Add the remaining ingredients. Stir. Heat through. Serves 4. Double the recipe to serve 8.

Carrot Combo

Carrot and a smaller amount of turnip are cooked together, then mashed together. Pictured on page 111.

1.	Water		
	Peeled and sliced carrots	3 cups	750 mL
	Peeled and cubed yellow turnip	1 cup	250 mL
	Salt	½ tsp.	2 mL
	Granulated sugar	½ tsp.	2 mL

You will need: measuring cups, a medium saucepan, measur-ing spoons, a sharp knife and a potato masher.

1. Pour enough water into the saucepan to be 1 inch (2.5 cm) deep. Add the carrots, turnip, salt and sugar. Cover. Bring to a boil on medium-high. Turn the heat down so it will simmer slow-ly about 20 minutes until the knife can easily pierce the pieces. Drain. Mash well. Sprinkle with some salt and pepper if need-ed. Serves 4.

Creamy Peas

So quick. Simply coating peas with sour cream is a snap.

1. Frozen peas (10 oz., 284 g)	**2½ cups**	**625 mL**
Water	**½ cup**	**125 mL**
Chicken bouillon powder	**½ tsp.**	**2 mL**
2. Sour cream	**4 tbsp.**	**60 mL**
Salt, sprinkle		
Pepper, sprinkle		

You will need: measuring spoons, measuring cups, a small saucepan and a mixing spoon.

1. Place the peas, water and bouillon powder in the saucepan. Stir. Cover. Bring to a boil on medium heat. Turn the heat down so it will simmer very slowly for 3 minutes. Drain well.

2. Add the sour cream. Stir the peas to coat them. Return the saucepan to the burner. Heat through on low. Taste to see if it needs a sprinkle of salt and pepper. Stir. Makes 4 servings.

Pictured below.

1. Carrot Combo page 110
2. Saucy Corn page 110
3. Creamy Peas

Dishes Courtesy Of:
The Bay Home Furnishings Dept.

Soap Bubbles

If you want a smaller amount, cut this recipe in half. Extremely easy to make. Do not freeze.

1. **Liquid dishwashing soap (green** ½ cup   125 mL
        makes colorful bubbles)
        Water   2½ cups   575 mL
        Glycerin (buy at the drug store)   1 tbsp.   15 mL
        Granulated sugar   1½ tsp.   7 mL

You will need: measuring spoons, measuring cups, a container with a lid and a mixing spoon.

1. Place all the ingredients into the container. Stir well. Cover and you have your solution. Make a ring out of twist ties or some wire. Dip into the solution and blow out bubbles. Makes 3 cups (675 mL).

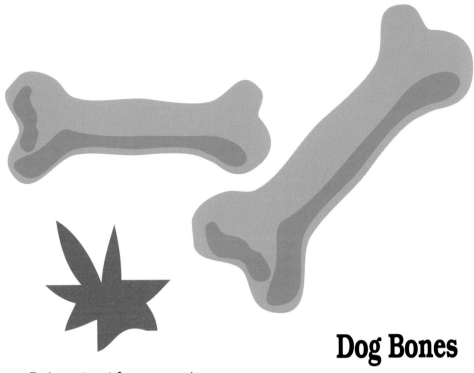

Dog Bones

Bake a treat for your pet.

1. All-purpose flour	**2 cups**	**500 mL**
Cornmeal	**1 cup**	**250 mL**
Wheat germ	**¼ cup**	**50 mL**
Beef bouillon powder	**2 tsp.**	**10 mL**
Garlic powder	**½ tsp.**	**2 mL**
2. Large egg	**1**	**1**
Cooking oil	**1 tbsp.**	**15 mL**
Hot water	**1 cup**	**250 mL**

You will need: measuring spoons, measuring cups, a medium bowl, a mixing spoon, a rolling pin, a cookie sheet, a cookie cutter, oven mitts and a wire rack.

1. Turn the oven on to 275°F (140°C). Combine the first 5 ingredients in the bowl. Stir.

2. Add the egg, cooking oil and water. Stir well. Roll out on a well-floured surface to a ½ inch (1 cm) thickness. Cut into bone shapes or other shapes. Arrange on the ungreased cookie sheet. Bake on the center rack in the oven for about 2 hours until dry and very hard. Use the oven mitts to remove the cookie sheet to the wire rack. Cool. Let stand overnight to dry thoroughly. Store in a container with a lid. Makes 10 big dog bones and 14 puppy bones.

Play Dough, Uncooked

Stays soft for several months. Do not freeze.

1.			
All-purpose flour		2½ cups	625 mL
Salt		½ cup	125 mL
Cooking oil		3 tbsp.	45 mL
Alum (from drugstore)		1 tbsp.	15 mL
Food coloring		¼ tsp.	1 mL
2. Boiling water		2 cups	500 mL

You will need: measuring spoons, measuring cups, a large bowl, a mixing spoon and a tea kettle.

1. Measure the first 5 ingredients into the bowl. Stir a bit.

2. Pour the boiling water carefully into the bowl. Stir well until it is too difficult to stir any more. Turn the dough out onto the counter, scraping the sides of the bowl. Gather it into a ball and knead the dough until it is smooth. Store in a plastic bag. Seal the bag tightly. Return the dough to the bag after each use. Do not eat. Makes about 3 cups (750 mL).

Pictured below.

Dough Art

Try your hand at some artistic works. Long lasting. Do not freeze.

1. **Recipe for Uncooked Play**   1   1
       Dough, without added food
       coloring, page 114

2. **Acrylic paints or water colors**
       Spray can of varnish or shellac

You will need: a rolling pin, cookie cutters, a cookie sheet and paint brushes.

1. Follow the recipe to make Uncooked Play Dough. Do not add food coloring. After kneading the dough, roll it out to ¼ inch (0.5 cm) thickness. Cut with cookie cutters. To air-dry, put cut-outs on cookie sheet. Let stand on the counter at room temperature for 48 to 72 hours until they are very dry. To hurry the process, bake on the center rack in a 300°F (150°C) oven for 45 to 60 minutes until golden brown. If you want to hang the cut-outs, either make a hole in the top using a straw, or stick in a hook made from a paper clip. Do this before baking or drying.

2. Paint with acrylic or water colors. Finish both sides with several coats of varnish.

Pictured below.

Bag Lunches

A standard, healthy bag lunch should contain a grain product, some fruit or vegetables, a milk product or a dairy product and meat or meat alternative. Add something extra for energy needs and as a special treat. To save time in the morning, prepare your lunch the night before and refrigerate it.

There are snacks, cookies, candy, squares and bread recipes in this book that could be included in your lunch bag. Also, check the Sandwich section, pages 84 to 89, for a variety of sandwich and sandwich filling recipes. Combine these with the Bread choices chart on page 118 and you will never get bored.

Consider how to keep meat and milk products cold. If you place a carton of frozen juice in the bottom of your lunch bag, it will keep your meat or fish sandwich safe to eat until lunchtime and makes a nice slushy drink. A small freezer pack works well, too, or try the following:

FROZEN GRAPES: Freeze a handful of seedless red or green grapes in a plastic container or bag. Include them in your lunch. They will still be cold when it's lunchtime.

FROZEN ORANGES: Cut an orange into quarters. Put them into a plastic container or bag. Freeze. Include them in your lunch.

FROZEN BANANA: Peel. Cut in half crosswise. Insert a flat wooden popsicle stick into the cut end, about half way into each half. Place each in a plastic container or bag. Freeze. Include one in your lunch.

Use the chart on pages 118 and 119 to help you decide what to put in your lunch. Build your bag lunch using the food on hand in the kitchen or plan ahead and add necessary items to the next grocery shopping list. As you think of, or try items not listed on those pages 118 and 119, write them in the blanks. Have fun bringing it all together! And don't forget to add a paper napkin or a paper towel. Use plastic, reusable containers if you can rather than plastic wrap or plastic bags.

1. Carrot And Celery Sticks
2. Stick Dip page 120
3. Ham And Cheese Sandwich page 84
4. Fresh Fruit
5. Ginger Crinkles page 37

Bag Lunch Suggestions

BREADS	FRUIT	VEGETABLES
Bagels	Apple	Alfalfa Sprouts
Baking Powder Biscuits	Banana	Asparagus
Breadsticks	Blueberries	Broccoli
Buns:	Cantaloupe	Carrot Sticks
Dinner Roll	Fruit Juice	Cauliflower
Hamburger Bun	Fruit Salad *	Celery Sticks
Hot Dog Bun	Grapefruit Sections	Cherry Tomatoes
Kaiser Roll	Grapes	Cucumber
Submarine Bun	Kiwifruit	Green Beans
Croissants	Melon	Lettuce
Lefsa	Nectarine	Radishes
Loaves:	Orange	Salad Lunch *
Cheese	Peach	Tomatoes
80% Whole Wheat	Pear	Vegetable Juices
Enriched Whites	Plums	Zucchini
100% Whole Wheat	Raspberries	
Raisin	Strawberries	
Rye		
7-Grain		
60% Whole Wheat		
Melba Toast		
Muffins:		
English Muffin		
Germ Muffins *		
Pitas		
Scones		
Soft Pretzels		
Tortillas		

* Recipe is included in this book.
See Index.

Bag Lunch Suggestions

MILK PRODUCTS	MEAT & ALTERNATIVES	EXTRAS
Cheese:	Cold Cooked Chicken/	Cake
Cheddar	Turkey Parts	Cookies:
Gouda	Hard-boiled Egg *	Butterscotch Oat Drops *
Mozzarella	Jerky:	Chocolate Oat Chippers *
Slices	Beef *	Ginger Crinkles *
Cottage Cheese	Ham *	Hermits *
Milk:	Turkey *	Jumbo Raisin Cookies *
Homogenized	Sandwich Fillings:	Peanut Butter Gems *
2%	Cheese *	Sugar Cookies *
1%	Cheese & Lettuce *	Dried Fruit
Skim	Cheese & Tomato *	Drinks:
Yogurt (Plain)	Chicken *	Chocolate Milk
	Deli Meats	Lemonade
_____	Egg *	Fruit Leather *
	Ham & Cheese *	Fruit Yogurt
_____	Ham & Lettuce *	Fun Buns *
	Ham & Tomato *	Peanut Chew *
_____	Peanut Butter *	Popcorn
	Peanut Butter &	Raisins
_____	Banana *	Squares:
	Salmon *	Brownies *
	Tuna *	Crisp Crunchies *
	Turkey	Crispy Rice Squares *
		Crispy Squares *
	_____	Crunchy Fudge *
		Puffed Wheat Squares *
	_____	Trail Mix *
	_____	_____
	_____	_____
		_____
		_____

* Recipe is included in this book.
See Index.

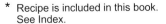

Salad Lunch

A bit of a crunch and all your favorite foods. Do not freeze.

1.			
	Lettuce chunks	2	2
	Tomato wedges	2	2
	Cucumber slices	3	3
	Celery stick	1	1
	Medium Cheddar cheese cubes	2	2
	Thin carrot sticks	3	3
	Hard-boiled egg, see page 81	½	½

You will need: a small plastic container with a lid.

1. Put all pieces gently into the container. Seal with the lid. Add a container of Stick Dip, recipe below, or your favorite salad dressing.

Pictured on page 117.

Stick Dip

A quick-to-make dip for a bag lunch that includes breadsticks or raw vegetables or crackers.

1.			
	Sour cream	3 tbsp.	45 mL
	Beef bouillon powder	½ tsp.	2 mL
	Onion salt	¼ tsp.	1 mL

You will need: measuring spoons, a small bowl, a mixing spoon and a small container with a lid.

1. Put the sour cream, bouillon powder and onion salt in the bowl. Mix well. Put into the container. Seal with the lid. Makes 3 tbsp. (45 mL).

Pictured on page 117.

Fruit Salad

So colorful, juicy and tasty. Choose from a variety of fresh fruits available at your grocery store. Do not freeze.

1. **Watermelon chunks**   6   6
    Kiwifruit slices, cut in half   3   3
    Cantaloupe chunks   4   4
    Orange segments, cut in half   3   3
    Seedless grapes, red or green,   6   6
        or both
    Apple or pear slices, or both,   3   3
        dipped in fruit juice or lemon
        juice to keep from browning

You will need: a plastic container with a lid.

1. Combine all ingredients in the container. Seal with the lid.

Pictured below.

Measurement Tables

Throughout this book measurements are given in Conventional and Metric measure. The cup used is the standard 8 fluid ounce. Temperature is given in degrees Fahrenheit and Celsius. Baking pan measurements are in inches and centimetres as well as quarts and litres.

Spoons

Conventional Measure	Metric Standard Measure Millilitre (mL)
¼ teaspoon (tsp.)	1 mL
½ teaspoon (tsp.)	2 mL
1 teaspoon (tsp.)	5 mL
2 teaspoons (tsp.)	10 mL
1 tablespoon (tbsp.)	15 mL

Cups

Conventional Measure	Metric Standard Measure Millilitre (mL)
¼ cup (4 tbsp.)	50 mL
⅓ cup (5⅓ tbsp.)	75 mL
½ cup (8 tbsp.)	125 mL
⅔ cup (10⅔ tbsp.)	150 mL
¾ cup (12 tbsp.)	175 mL
1 cup (16 tbsp.)	250 mL
4 cups	1000 mL (1 L)

Weight Measurements

Ounces (oz.)	Grams (g)
1 oz.	30 g
2 oz.	55 g
3 oz.	85 g
4 oz.	125 g
5 oz.	140 g
6 oz.	170 g
7 oz.	200 g
8 oz.	250 g
16 oz.	500 g
32 oz.	1000 g (1 kg)

Oven Temperatures

Fahrenheit (°F)	Celsius (°C)
175°	80°
200°	95°
225°	110°
250°	120°
275°	140°
300°	150°
325°	160°
350°	175°
375°	190°
400°	205°
425°	220°
450°	230°
475°	240°
500°	260°

Pans

Conventional Inches	Metric Centimetres
8x8 inch	20x20 cm
9x9 inch	22x22 cm
9x13 inch	22x33 cm
10x15 inch	25x38 cm
11x17 inch	28x43 cm
8x2 inch round	20x5 cm
9x2 inch round	22x5 cm
10x4½ inch tube	25x11 cm
8x4x3 inch loaf	20x10x7 cm
9x5x3 inch loaf	22x12x7 cm

Casseroles

Conventional Quart (qt.)	Metric Litre (L)
1 qt.	1.2 L
1¼ qt.	1.5 L
1⅔ qt.	2 L
2 qt.	2.5 L
3⅓ qt.	4 L
4¼ qt.	5 L

Index

MAIL ORDER COUPON
Save $5.00!
Deduct $5.00 for every $35.00 ordered

ENGLISH

QUANTITY • COMPANY'S COMING SERIES

	150 Delicious Squares		Cakes
	Casseroles		Barbecues
	Muffins & More		Dinners of the World
	Salads		Lunches
	Appetizers		Pies
	Desserts		Light Recipes
	Soups & Sandwiches		Microwave Cooking
	Holiday Entertaining		Preserves
	Cookies		Light Casseroles
	Vegetables		Chicken, Etc.
	Main Courses		NEW Kids Cooking
	Pasta		NEW Fish & Seafood (April '96)

NO. OF BOOKS **PRICE**

$10.95 + $1.50 shipping = **$12.45 each** x [ ] = $ [ ]

QUANTITY • PINT SIZE BOOKS

	Finger Food		Baking Delights
	Party Planning		NEW Chocolate (October '95)
	Buffets		

NO. OF BOOKS **PRICE**

$4.99 + $1.00 shipping = **$5.99 each** x [ ] = $ [ ]

FRENCH

QUANTITY • JEAN PARÉ LIVRES DE CUISINE

	150 délicieux carrés		Les salades
	Les casseroles		La cuisson au micro-ondes
	Muffins et plus		Les pâtes
	Les dîners		Les conserves
	Les barbecues		Les casseroles légères
	Les tartes		Poulet, etc.
	Délices des fêtes		NEW La cuisine pour les enfants
	Recettes légères		NEW Poissons et fruits de mer (avril '96)

NO. OF BOOKS **PRICE**

$10.95 + $1.50 shipping = **$12.45 each** x [ ] = $ [ ]

TOTAL

- **MAKE CHEQUE OR MONEY ORDER PAYABLE TO:** *COMPANY'S COMING PUBLISHING LIMITED*
- **ORDERS OUTSIDE CANADA:** *Must be paid in U.S. funds by cheque or money order drawn on Canadian or U.S. bank.*
- *Prices subject to change without prior notice.*
- *Sorry, no C.O.D.'s*

TOTAL PRICE FOR ALL BOOKS	$
Less $5.00 for every $35.00 ordered −	$
SUBTOTAL	$
Canadian residents add G.S.T. +	$
TOTAL AMOUNT ENCLOSED	$

Please complete shipping address on reverse.

Gift Giving

- Let us help you with your gift giving!

- We will send cookbooks directly to the recipients of your choice if you give us their names and addresses.

- Be sure to specify the titles you wish to send to each person.

- If you would like to include your personal note or card, we will be pleased to enclose it with your gift order.

- Company's Coming Cookbooks make excellent gifts. Birthdays, bridal showers, Mother's Day, Father's Day, graduation or any occasion... collect them all!

Shipping address

Send the Company's Coming Cookbooks listed on the reverse side of this coupon, to:

Name:

Street:

City: Province/State:

Postal Code/Zip: Tel: (   )   —

COOKBOOKS

Company's Coming Publishing Limited
Box 8037, Station F
Edmonton, Alberta, Canada T6H 4N9
Tel: (403) 450-6223